Praise for *Jane the Virgin*

"This nuanced exploration of *Jane the Virgin*—'a true TV milestone' in Paul Julian Smith's words—will appeal to scholars, students, and fans alike. Taking into account production context, narrative structure and social themes, genre, and stars, Smith combines engaging and intricate analysis with ludic insights about his own viewing experience of this award-winning show."

—Fiona Noble, lecturer in Spanish and Latin American studies, University of Stirling

"In this masterful study, Paul Julian Smith demonstrates why *Jane the Virgin* matters to US and Latin American audiences. Smith's writing is approachable to specialists and fans and to casual readers who may have heard of the show but never fully entered its fandom. You'll want to binge-watch the show after reading this book!"

—Vinodh Venkatesh, professor of Spanish, Virginia Tech

"Drawing on conventional scholarly approaches and fan sources, Paul Julian Smith maps out a nuanced, learned, and engagingly written analysis of the popular series *Jane the Virgin*. This is a vital contribution for those interested in the series and the growing presence of Latinas across streaming platforms."

—Niamh Thornton, professor in Latin American studies, University of Liverpool

"Writing as a scholar as well as a self-confessed fan, Paul Julian Smith provides an acutely observed and detailed account of this highly popular drama. Its particular appeal lies in the balance of context with nuanced and beautifully written textual analysis. This book is as engaging as it is rigorous and will delight fans, students, and scholars alike."

—Abigail Loxham, reader in Hispanic film studies, University of Liverpool

Jane the Virgin

TV Milestones

Series Editor

Barry Keith Grant, Brock University

TV Milestones is part of the Contemporary Approaches to Film and Media Series.

A complete listing of the books in this series can be found online at wsupress.wayne.edu.

Jane the Virgin

Paul Julian Smith

Wayne State University Press
Detroit

ISBN 9780814352618 (paperback)
ISBN 9780814352625 (ebook)

Library of Congress Control Number: 2025931232

Published with the assistance of a fund established by Thelma Gray James of Wayne State University for the publication of folklore and English studies.

Wayne State University Press rests on Waawiyaataanong, also referred to as Detroit, the ancestral and contemporary homeland of the Three Fires Confederacy. These sovereign lands were granted by the Ojibwe, Odawa, Potawatomi, and Wyandot Nations, in 1807, through the Treaty of Detroit. Wayne State University Press affirms Indigenous sovereignty and honors all tribes with a connection to Detroit. With our Native neighbors, the press works to advance educational equity and promote a better future for the earth and all people.

Wayne State University Press
Leonard N. Simons Building
4809 Woodward Avenue
Detroit, Michigan 48201-1309

Visit us online at wsupress.wayne.edu.

CONTENTS

ACKNOWLEDGMENTS

First of all, I thank the CUNY Graduate Center and its Comparative Literature Program, especially Executive Officer Giancarlo Lombardi and Deputy Executive Officer Bettina Lerner, for creating such a fruitful and productive environment for my research. One of the program's many excellent PhD students, Coco Fitterman, was responsible for compiling the meticulous list of works cited at the end of this book.

It is a huge pleasure to return to Wayne State University Press, where I previously published *Queer Mexico: Cinema and Television Since 2000*, and where I am most indebted to Marie Sweetman, the senior acquisitions editor, for her kindness, efficiency, and encouragement. I also thank Barry Keith Grant, the series editor of TV Milestones, and the two anonymous readers for their attentive and helpful comments.

I am of course immensely grateful to the creative team that made *Jane the Virgin*, especially Jennie Snyder Urman and Gina Rodriguez, for one hundred delightful, skillful, and thought-provoking episodes. Finally, I thank the superfans of *Jane the Virgin*, who so kindly and generously responded with their comments when I posted on Reddit that I was writing this book. Surely few television series have inspired such a faithful and positive fan community, and few are as worthy of that devotion as *Jane the Virgin*.

INTRODUCTION

"It Should Be Noted . . ."

Jane the Virgin is a unique hybrid comedy-drama-telenovela parody that was shown free to air on minor network The CW over five seasons and one hundred episodes from 2014–19 and is at the time of writing still streaming at full length on Netflix. It boasts the unlikely premise of the accidental insemination of a sexually inexperienced girl in Miami. The show was a fan favorite among eighteen-to-thirty-five-year-old women, the target demographic of the broadcaster, and its pilot attracted an audience of over one million viewers. It was also a major award winner, gaining not only the Golden Globe for best actress for its protagonist, breakout star Gina Rodriguez, but also a rare and prestigious Peabody for its contribution to broadcasting more generally. It also won Imagen Awards for its positive depiction of Latinx characters.

This weekly long-form series is a true TV milestone, and the proof lies not only in its innovative narrative form (which includes an omniscient Narrator, who intermittently comments on the action and is known as Latin Lover and voiced by Anthony Mendez) but in its engagement with and depiction of a Spanish-heritage-language minority and its focus on issues vital to this group, such as immigration status, citizenship, and access to health care. Such protagonists are still underrepresented in US mainstream television. Most unusually for a prime-time US broadcast drama, *Jane the Virgin* also includes in every episode some dialogue in Spanish, spoken by the main character's abuela Alba ("Dawn"), played by veteran Ivonne Coll, who will not be heard to say a word of English until "Chapter Twenty." In addition to fondly parodying telenovelas and featuring an established Mexican actor (Jaime Camil) who is a veteran of such serials in his home country, *Jane the Virgin* is also the sole successful US adaptation of a Venezuelan example of the genre, *Juana la virgen* (RCTV, 2002). The only comparable phenomenon is its equally loved and groundbreaking predecessor, ABC's *Ugly Betty* (2006–10), which was based, also loosely, on a celebrated Colombian original (*Yo soy Betty, la fea* ["I Am Ugly Betty," RCN, 1999–2001]).

Proof of *Jane the Virgin*'s continuing influence and significance in the world of television is that it has itself spawned local format deals with countries such as China, Korea, and Israel (Tartaglione 2019). The Venezuelan original also inspired a Mexican–US version (the euphemistically named *La historia de Juana* ["Juana's Story"]) that premiered on TelevisaUnivision as late as June 3, 2024. The CW's *Jane the Virgin* may be frothy fun, with its Day-Glo decor and wardrobe and its sun-drenched exteriors, but it is also serious business both for its expert creative team, led by distinguished showrunner Jennie Snyder Urman, and its still-devoted audience, who continue to post on social media years after its finale. Additionally, its assured tone combines in a tricky equilibrium campy humor and heartfelt drama.

In the new streaming era, *Jane the Virgin* has now taken on added value as one of the last and most successful old-style broadcast series, capable of captivating a mass audience week after week over half a decade. When the hitherto secretive Netflix tardily released an annual viewership report in December 2023, it was discovered that the series had garnered an extraordinary 180.7 million hours on the platform.

As the *Washington Post* observed in two crossover comments on Netflix's statistics that work well for *Jane the Virgin*: "shows about women struggling to make it performed strikingly well"; and "Latinos are attracting massive audiences" (Loofbourow 2023).

This book is divided into an introduction, four chapters, and a conclusion. The first chapter, "Televisual Histories," traces *Jane the Virgin*'s unique production process and tracks its reception in the press (both general and trade) and by the audience (on social media) in the USA and abroad. The second chapter is called "Text and Context." It explores the complex narrative structure of the series over its five seasons and its social themes, especially feminist, Latinx, and queer issues. Chapter 3 is "Generic Affiliation / Family Filiation" and examines *Jane the Virgin*'s contradictory relationship with telenovelas, which it both fondly references and archly parodies. Finally, the fourth chapter examines "Stars and Performance," focusing on the persona and acting style of protagonist Gina Rodriguez and her supporting cast. These discursive chapters are interspersed with close readings of five episodes of the series, vital season premieres and finales, which I call "Intermissions." They tease out the connections between aesthetics, thematics, and politics, which are explored more broadly in the chapters themselves. They also aim to recreate the experience of watching the series, with all its associated visual and narrative pleasures, for readers who may be unfamiliar with or forgetful of it.

This book, then, makes a fan's fond and admiring case for *Jane the Virgin* as a TV milestone. But it also calls critical attention to the paradoxes in the series' premise: a rare but assured blend of comedy and tragedy, Anglo and Latinx, escapist romance and disconcerting realism.

INTERMISSION 1
THE PILOT ("CHAPTER ONE")

Jane with mother Xiomara at the clinic.

Rafael with wife Petra.

Doctor Luisa, Xiomara, and Jane at the clinic.

Jane with fiancé Michael at the celebratory lunch gone wrong.

It's 9:00 p.m. Eastern (8:00 p.m. Central) on October 13, 2014. Turn on your TV set and seek out The CW on your cable menu.

The inaugural episode of *Jane the Virgin* is referred to as a chapter, a direct nod to its allegiance to the Spanish word for "episode": *capítulo*. It commences with a cold open, an unannounced precredit sequence that is labeled a "prologue." A Latin-accented male voice-over, soon to become very familiar to the newly loyal audience, declares, "Our story begins." The scene starts with an extreme close-up of the flawless white petals of a flower, accompanied by a young, wide-eyed Jane at the age of ten. On-screen titles, accompanied by the sound of a clicking keyboard, succinctly encapsulate the passions that define the as-yet-unknown characters. For Jane, these passions are family, faith, and (in a very American twist) grilled cheese sandwiches. The passions of her grandmother Alba, on the other hand, revolve around faith and Jane herself.

The initial dialogue is in subtitled Spanish, featuring the stern lecture of the grandmother instructing the young girl to crumple the blossom in her hand. The moral is evident: Just like the irreversible loss of one's virginity, once you destroy a perfect, pure flower, it can never be restored. However, this conservative, explicitly Catholic viewpoint is immediately challenged. Jane's mother, the alluring Xiomara, played by Andrea Navedo, whose passions include Jane and the Mexican singing star Paulina Rubio (a future guest on the show who will appear in "Chapter Nine"), is depicted skeptically painting her nails while the grandmother lectures the girl. While Jane will dress modestly, Xiomara ("Xo") will favor glittery miniskirts and what she calls booty shorts.

This is an all-female household, symbolizing a new environment for Latinas, as indicated by the characters' surname "Villanueva" (literally "new town," an appropriate name for immigrants). In a seamless transition, when the crumpled flower falls to the floor, the show cuts to precisely thirteen and a half years later, where the same damaged blossom is framed on the wall behind Jane's bed. Now played by star Gina Rodriguez, Jane is engaged in a passionate embrace, albeit fully clothed, with her light-brown-haired, blue-eyed boyfriend Michael, played by Canadian Brett Dier (who seems to be Anglo, although his surname is of Spanish origin: Cordero). When things get too steamy, she abruptly stops him in his tracks. Jane, with a heart-shaped face, dark eyes, a sprinkling of freckles, and a softly rounded body, represents a fresh face on American network television. A simple title card now appears on the screen and there is no credit sequence. This fast pace will be characteristic of the series to come.

The home shared by the three women (daughter Jane, mother Xiomara, and grandmother Alba) is a one-story, whitewashed house furnished with colorful, comfortable furniture and a swing on the porch, which is primed for intimate, late-night discussions. The low ceiling and subdued lighting reveal a relatively realistic setting. Now a song titled "Una flor" ("A Flower") begins to play. It is sung by Colombian superstar Juanes, who will make a cameo as a music producer in

"Chapter Eight." It should be noted that the lyrics, which are clearly relevant to the plot, are left untranslated, making them inaccessible to an English-speaking audience. In contrast, all Spanish dialogue is subtitled. We soon learn that the song, seemingly nondiegetic (that is, coming from outside the story space), actually emanates from the old-fashioned television set in the characters' home, thus blurring the lines between everyday life and the media landscape. Seated comfortably on a single couch, the three women watch a telenovela side by side. On screen, Rogelio de la Vega (expertly played by Mexican TV star Jaime Camil), resplendent in a lavender blazer, kisses his beloved on the prow of a flagrantly fake boat before a green-screen sunset.

In a second seamless visual transition, the camera glides from the simulated water on Rogelio's television serial over the real-life ocean in front of fashionable South Beach's high-rise buildings. They are tantalizingly close yet distant from Jane's modest, low-rise neighborhood (the Narrator tells us the new location is exactly "8.2 miles away"). An outdoor scene unfolds at night, situated by the swimming pool of the Marbella, the luxury hotel newly owned by the darkly handsome Rafael, played by Justin Baldoni (who makes his shirtless debut just sixteen minutes into the episode).

This location displays a well-crafted example of production design, as the billowing aqua drapes match the water in the hotel pool. The on-screen titles label Rafael's blond wife Petra (Yael Grobglas) as a "man-eater," and as she kneels before her husband, the titles and actions none too subtly imply oral sex. The graphic content continues in the subsequent scene, with coworker Lina (Diane Guerrero) skeptically asking Jane in the locker room why she has not intimately connected ("boned") with her longtime boyfriend Michael. To complicate matters still further, Jane is working for Rafael, who will prove to be her unsuspecting sperm donor, and has at some time previously shared a single romantic kiss with him.

The subsequent sequence epitomizes *Jane the Virgin*'s tricky tone. Having literally drawn a short straw with her fellow workers, Jane, in an absurd but endearing twist, is dressed as a mermaid to serve drinks at the hotel. In a moment of pure physical comedy, she flops into the pool to avoid encountering Rafael, resulting in a sight gag with her tail flapping as she moves away. This comic sequence also leads into the requisite romantic encounter ("meet cute" [or, more properly, "remeet cute"]) for the couple (this phrase will be explained on-screen in "Chapter Thirty-Two"). Back in the hotel bar, we witness an endearing reunion for the future lovers. Playboy Rafael has not quite forgotten his previous magical kiss with a younger Jane and remarks to the dripping waitress, "You seem familiar." Later he will be the first character to take Jane's ambition to be a creative writer seriously, telling her, "Be brave." The romantic acoustic guitar theme that sounds here is composed by Oscar-winner Gustavo Santaolalla, who became celebrated for his score for Mexican Alejandro González Iñárritu's *Amores perros* back in 2000. His contribution to *Jane the Virgin* is a small example of the new infusion of talent from independent Latin American film into quality US television.

Despite these transparent class differences and the beginnings of a love triangle (classic telenovela elements), the sophisticated Miami setting goes well beyond the confines of traditional melodrama. Surprisingly, perhaps, Rafael fondly instructs his sister Luisa, played by Yara Martinez, who is also present in the hotel bar, to return to "her wife." Lesbianism is here taken as a matter of fact within the fictional world but is qualified by a noteworthy political reference in the scene's titles: Rafael's sister is pointedly described as being "married in some states" (the pilot was filmed prior to the US Supreme Court's nationwide marriage equality decision). Rafael's sister also happens to be the doctor who, distressed and distracted by her spouse's infidelity, mistakenly performs the insemination just ten minutes into the pilot. A drowsy and inattentive Jane had attended the clinic anticipating a simple pap smear.

Jane's doctor realizes her mistake immediately, as her sister-in-law Petra is waiting in the next room, futilely expecting the lost, sole sample. The now-healthy Rafael has survived a bout with cancer that has left him infertile. Jane's storyline is thus already accelerated and intensified by the close connections between the main characters. At this juncture, the Narrator pronounces that Jane's life has turned into the "stuff of telenovela"—but in reality, it has not quite. As we shall see, the series' highly colored opening deviates significantly from the relative austerity and simplicity of the original Venezuelan serial known as *Juana la virgen*. The American show defines telenovela through a campy extravagance that is in fact relatively absent in its graver Latin American model.

Two weeks later, in fictional time, we find mother and daughter in an everyday working-class setting: the bus, which is Jane's primary mode of transportation. Yet when Jane is informed of her inexplicable pregnancy, in a moment of "magical realism," a term often invoked by the series' creator, telenovela star Rogelio appears in the clinic, donning the same lavender blazer and flashing the same cheesy smile seen on TV. He reassures her in Spanish that everything will be fine. The wardrobe also plays a significant role here: unlike the dapper Rogelio, Jane wears a plain jean jacket. Later a poster of Rogelio will wink conspiratorially at Jane as she once more rides her bus, a gesture repeated by Jane herself in the very last episode, the series finale. *Jane the Virgin* is thus simultaneously believable and unbelievable, invoking alternately the heightened reality characteristic of telenovela and the everyday ambience more typical of the US series genre. Newly minted star Gina Rodriguez employs her intelligence, wide-eyed charm, and natural-looking appearance to carry the audience beyond the series' controversial premise and title.

Characteristic of this grounded realism is the pilot's frank discussion of pregnancy termination and reproductive rights. Jane's mother Xiomara offers her the pills she could use for an abortion but imposes no pressure, explicitly stating, "You have a choice." Although Jane suspects that her own mother had contemplated abortion, we discover that it was in fact the devout grandmother Alba who, twenty-three years before, had requested Jane's mother abort. Loving her granddaughter as she does now, the grandmother is deeply ashamed of her past request. Addressing the niche young female audience who can locate the little-known channel of The CW on their cable lineup, an audience very conscious of their reproductive health, the series can afford here to add complexity to its characters, both psychologically and ethically. It does so in some unexpected ways. Surprisingly, in the next turn of events, it is tender and patient Michael, Jane's Anglo fiancé, who suggests aborting the child, who doesn't fit into the future life he and Jane have so carefully planned together.

In this context of carefully managed ambivalence, direct conflicts between characters are downplayed. Jane's mother and grandmother get along well most of the time; and, deferring to traditional Catholic practice, all three women are shown attending mass together. Jane may argue with her unmarried mother, who has long aspired to be a singing star, but she is rueful about their close relationship, saying sadly, "I derailed her life." The last major plot point in the pilot is the unlikely revelation that Rogelio, the TV star adored from afar by the three women, was once the teenage boyfriend of Jane's mother. Crucially, he is also Jane's father, whom she has never met.

This unexpected twist is coupled with the intense visual pleasure also typical of a telenovela. When, in a final sequence of gender reversal, Jane, clad in a buttercup yellow dress and perilous high heels, proposes marriage to Michael on her knees, another pure white flower falls ominously from her hair. This symbolically harks back to the opening sequence when the crumpled flower fell from young Jane's hand. Despite the narrative complexities I have charted here, then, it will also be the art design that propels Jane's story, creating memorable graphic matches and color effects lodged in the audience's memory. The final title card of the series' first episode (or chapter) humorously states, "To be continued." In reality, as fans now know so well, the pilot would be swiftly picked up by The CW. And *Jane the Virgin*, a rare and delicate blossom on US network TV, would last for five seasons and a full one hundred episodes.

1
TELEVISUAL HISTORIES

This chapter provides an in-depth analysis of the production process of *Jane the Virgin*, contextualizing it within the challenges faced by its minor network, The CW, as it struggled to connect with a young female audience. Despite being described by its Anglo executive producer in universal terms as "one family's story" (Miller 2016, 9), the show ensured it had new writers from Latin America on its team to avoid perpetuating stereotypes. The chapter also explores the reception of the series in the press and on social media, both in the USA and abroad. In Venezuela, viewers anticipated the return of their cherished national TV heritage in a different format and with a more significant budget, while in Mexico fans focused on the prominent role of a much-loved local star.

Characteristically, *Jane the Virgin* incorporates what *Variety* will call ironic yet warm metacommentary on TV production processes (Lowry 2014). For example, after shooting the finale of his first (fictional) telenovela in the Miami studios, star Rogelio thanks each of the numerous crew members in turn, with typical inadvertent humor: the grips for their gripping, the gaffers for their gaffes, the best boy for being simply the best ("Chapter Twenty-Eight"). Or again in "Chapter Forty-Three," inspired by Rogelio's version of labor organizer César Chávez in his later time-travel telenovela ("¡Sí se puede!" or "Yes, we can!"), the crew will go on strike, thus imperiling Jane's wedding reception, the venue of which Rogelio has had built on the soundstage by that same long-suffering crew.

When the first season, consisting of twenty-two hour-long episodes, premiered in 2013, it marked a twelve-year gap from the original Venezuelan version. Notably, The CW chose a direct English translation of the title, departing from the euphemistic "Juana's Miracle" that was previously used in references to the original telenovela in the American trade press. In spite of the differences between the two series, *Jane the Virgin* retains two classic telenovela tropes from *Juana la virgen*: the cross-class romance and the love triangle. In *Juana la virgen*, however, it is two women who compete for one wealthy man: there is no equivalent of loyal, middle-class Michael. And *Jane the Virgin* introduces additional layers of romantic complexity, absent in the original.

As we have seen, Jane is engaged to Michael, a police officer who understands no Spanish and who competes with the Latino inseminator, wealthy Rafael, Jane's employer. We also discover that Jane's mother long ago enjoyed a teenage relationship with the future telenovela star Rogelio, who turns out to be Jane's biological father. In a further intricate pattern of connections, the doctor responsible for Jane's insemination is both the lesbian sister of the donor and the former lover of red-haired Rose (Bridget Regan), who is now the wife of the magnate who is the father of both doctor and donor. Rose and Luisa, ex-lovers who are now stepmother and stepdaughter, share a very hot kiss as early as "Chapter Two."

Some of the most significant differences between the two series emerge from *Jane the Virgin* being set in Miami, a vital hub for telenovela production that is strategically positioned between the US and Latin America. The show incorporates parodic and ironic telenovela references into its narrative, including the running commentary of the off-screen voice-over and the presence of Jaime Camil and his character Rogelio. He is an established star whose current show is shot in Miami, the production having moved at his insistence from Mexico, as he wishes to be close to his daughter, Jane, whom he only discovered the existence of recently, and her mother. *Jane the Virgin* thus assumes a certain geographical and cultural distance that allows it to playfully comment on a Latin American media practice that takes itself very seriously in its own region and in the US on mass-market Spanish-language networks like Univision, which recently merged with Mexican behemoth Televisa.

Additionally, *Jane the Virgin* distinguishes itself by emphasizing the protagonist's ethnicity as a Latina, specifically a Venezuelan American. This is a departure from the original show, where the heroine's nationality need not be specified, as she is like the rest of the cast just another member of the local population of the Venezuelan capital, Caracas. Jane's abuela is a pious undocumented immigrant from Venezuela who fled to Miami with her once wealthy husband decades before. Despite the remake's emphasis on Catholicism (relatively absent in the original telenovela), Jane herself is deeply committed to feminist ideals, striving for women's autonomy and community from the beginning. It remains the case that she has promised her abuela as a child to wait for marriage before having sex, and a Catholic ceremony such as baptism is taken very seriously in "Chapter Twenty-Five" as a religious ritual that links generations of mothers and their children. The momentous church wedding in "Chapter Forty-Four" (my Intermission 3) is likewise taken quite seriously.

Beyond these surface-level differences, the narrative structure and tone pose intriguing challenges. When the US version premiered in Venezuela on the Lifetime cable channel, it was noted in the local press that the American protagonist, Jane, is twenty-three years old, deviating from the seventeen-year-old character Juana in the original Venezuelan version (Franceschi 2015). Furthermore, *Jane the Virgin* was classified as a comedy, while *Juana la virgen* was categorized as a drama. The American show nonetheless received acclaim in Venezuela for its genre-blending approach, encompassing elements of drama, comedy, and magical realism, striking a tonal balance that allowed it to address political considerations, such as abortion and reproductive rights, in a less serious manner than the original. Although *Jane the Virgin* was not allowed to compete for the Emmys as a drama, it has, thanks to star Rodriguez, many moments of genuinely affecting emotion. For example, Jane's brief but heartfelt monologue to her abuela on how, as a single mother, she must learn how to do everything on her own ("Chapter Twenty") was one of many scenes that brought me to unexpected tears.

The success of *Jane the Virgin* in attracting a broad US audience, particularly women and millennials, is attributed to its network's improved programming and better production quality. While at the time 17 percent of the US population was of Hispanic descent, only 3 percent of supporting film or TV roles were allocated to Latino men and 10 percent to Latinas (Suddath 2015, 76). The changing constituency of both the cinema and TV industries thus enabled minority storytelling, once more often confined to independent cinema, to become more feasible on network television.

We can now sketch in more detail the production process of *Jane the Virgin,* drawing on the varied accounts of the English-language trade journals (*The Hollywood Reporter* and *Variety*) and the general press (*The New York Times*) and national dailies in Mexico, the biggest Spanish American media market (*Milenio* and *El Universal*). We then turn to reception on two platforms: the still active Reddit discussion portal and the surprisingly professional wiki fandom site. The former boasted 35,500 "Villanuevas" (i.e., registered users) in January 2024, placing it in the top 5 percent of all subreddits. The members online at any given time are playfully described as being "at the Marbella," the show's fictional luxury hotel.

Front and center from the start in the specialist coverage is Jennie Snyder Urman, who will take multiple credits as executive producer, adapter, and sole writer of the vital pilot episode. On July 18, 2014, *The Hollywood Reporter* was surprised on a press tour for the forthcoming show that co-executive producer Ben Silverman contributed rather little to public discussion (O'Connell 2014). Although responsible for the somewhat similar telenovela adaption *Ugly Betty*, he allowed Urman to take credit for this new Latinx family dramedy. Citing "three generations" of women, Urman invoked as a perhaps unlikely inspiration for *Jane the Virgin* the very WASP series *Gilmore Girls*, which played on The CW's predecessor, The WB. She stressed the "tricky tone" of the new show, "less soapy" than the original Venezuelan serial but still an "ode to the telenovela." Hence her plan with the American version was to include some "extreme storylines" (such as "evil twins") for the sake of comedy, just so long as the main characters remain "grounded and relatable."

Additionally, the then little-known Gina Rodriguez was also voluble, "charm[ing] the room." Rodriguez claimed she passed on the stereotypical Latina-cast dramedy *Devious Maids* (Lifetime, 2013–16), saying that she wanted to "push forward the idea of my culture": "I wasn't going to let my introduction to the world be a story that's been told many times." A few months later, at the meeting of the National Association of Television Program Executives (NATPE) on January 2, 2015, Jorge Granier, managing director of the Venezuelan Radio Caracas Televisión (RCTV), which had made *Juana la virgen*, and now an executive producer on *Jane the Virgin*, described to *Variety* the industrial background to this newly transnational cultural content: "In Latin America we have amazing storytellers . . . Because there's such a big presence [of Latinx] in the US . . . it's only natural to make good enough adaptations to appeal to this broader, more diverse audience in the US" (O'Hare 2015). In addition, from season four, Gina Rodriguez herself would earn a credit as executive producer.

Another fortuitous but fortunate business trend at the time was the rise of comedy as a genre. *Variety* once more argues that although "a bracing series of classic dramas," including *Mad Men* (AMC, 2007–15) and *Breaking Bad* (AMC, 2008–13), were once the pride of TV's new golden age of the millennium, in the following decade, "Peak TV is Peak Comedy" (Ryan 2016). Moreover, *Jane the Virgin*, then in its second season, is "the best show on TV right now," according to Ryan, "skillfully weav[ing] together comedy, family drama, melodrama, and ironic yet warm meta-commentary." However, if the media zeitgeist seems to have changed, then once more there is an industrial subtext: newly booming comedies are sometimes cheaper to make than now-ailing prestige dramas. Significantly, Isabel Molina-Guzmán's excellent pioneering book *Latinas and Latinos on TV*, which briefly addresses *Jane the Virgin* in its conclusion (2018, Kindle location 1997–2021), focuses on the genre of sitcom, paying special attention to *Modern Family* (ABC, 2009–20), to which I will return later.

Typically, *Jane the Virgin* smartly satirizes this tendency too. Having been fired from his original show, the clueless Rogelio, now both star and executive producer, remakes *Mad Men* in Spanish as the (inadvertently) humorous telenovela *Hombres locos* ("Chapter Twenty-Eight")—that is, until he gets hit with a "cease and desist" letter from the creator of the original classic drama (Rogelio asks: "Who's Matthew Weiner?"). Weiner, seen only from behind, like Don Draper in his series' credits, is unmoved when Rogelio rushes to plead with him in Los Angeles. *Jane the Virgin* also skewers the UK prestige TV drama that was so acclaimed at the time. When Rogelio and his then-girlfriend Xiomara watch *Downton Abbey* together, he dismisses her favorite show: "This British telenovela is not so original. We did the Egyptian deflowering the virgin and dying in her bed on *Amor de Arabia*" ("Chapter Thirty-Five").

As if to prove *Variety*'s point of "peak comedy," when the second season of *Jane the Virgin* began, it was joined on The CW by another innovative, female-focused comic series. *Crazy Ex-Girlfriend* (2015–19) explored mental health issues via musical numbers reminiscent of classic Hollywood (later seasons of *Jane the Virgin* will also address mental health with some seriousness). In what *Variety*, on August 21, 2015, called a "nifty promotional campaign," Rodriguez posted a video of her mambo-tap routine in response to a dance challenge made by *Crazy Ex-Girlfriend*, with proceeds going to the charity Broadway Cares / Equity Fights AIDS (Friedlander 2015).

Along similar lines in the general press, *The New York Times* asked, "How is US TV changing?" and answered its own question: "Ask Jane" (Steel 2015). Here the focus is once more on new star Gina Rodriguez as a charismatic spokesperson for *Jane the Virgin*. In this article, her varied fans are said to include "a Hispanic teenager" working in a fast-food restaurant and "a white couple in their [sixties]" who are also the owners of a golf course. Now that there are 54 million people who "identify as Hispanic or Latino" in the US, "cross-cultural appeal," we are told, "can be good for [TV] business," with *Jane the Virgin* averaging over a million viewers in its first season and attracting critical acclaim. Rodriguez, meanwhile, who is said to "charm critics and TV executives alike," here chooses to play down the Latinx element of the story to the general press: "It's just a girl who wants a dream to come true." Incidentally, this "dream" is as professional as it is romantic: the long-running ambition of trainee teacher Jane to become a published writer.

It is something of a shock to shift focus to the press coverage of *Jane the Virgin* in Mexico, the biggest and most lucrative Spanish-speaking TV market. Here, as in Venezuela, the series was shown to a more select audience than in the US on cable channel Lifetime (in a later chapter we examine the question of dubbing this bilingual show for Spanish speakers in different countries). Keeping TV coverage in the family, as it were, the Mexican focus is almost exclusively on Jaime Camil, the cinema and telenovela actor who was already much loved at home. This is in spite of the fact that, although he does appear in every episode, Camil's Rogelio, the shallow TV star who is Jane's biological father, is clearly a supporting character in the series.

Early headlines in national broadsheet *El Universal* read in translation: "Camil and *Jane the Virgin* will arrive in Mexico" ("Camil y 'Jane the virgin' llegarán a México" 2015); "Camil and [Andrea] Navedo [who plays Jane's mother Xiomara] present *Jane the Virgin* in Mexico" (Navedo bravely tried out her nonnative Spanish at this press event) (Mérida 2015); "Camil will work with Britney Spears on *Jane the Virgin*"

(Huerta Ortiz 2015a); "Jaime Camil starts work on second season of *Jane the Virgin*" ("Jaime Camil arranca segunda temporada de 'Jane the virgin'" 2015); and even "Jaime Camil and [executive producer Ben] Silverman want to produce quality cinema and TV" ("Jaime Camil y Silverman quieren producir cine y TV de calidad" 2015).

The local actor is thus presented to Mexican audiences not just as the sole star of the show but also as a key creative contributor. Jaime Camil's ambitious professional journey from Mexico therefore parallels those of Latin American TV executives like Jorge Granier, who brought his series format from Venezuela to the US. This tendency for talent to move over to management is once more satirized within *Jane the Virgin* itself when, in "Chapter Twenty-Five," Rogelio is given a vanity credit as "EP" (executive producer) on his *novela The Passions of Santos*. He helpfully explains the title to his family: "It's like being a chief of police but with higher stakes."

Just as Gina Rodriguez needs to manage contradictory audience expectations in the US (promoting the "idea of [her] culture" to *Variety* yet claiming her character is "just a girl" to *The New York Times*), so Jaime Camil needs to address concerns in his native Mexico. Those viewers may see the cross-border migration of a cherished local star either negatively, as a betrayal of his home territory, or more positively, as a focus for national pride. It seems consensus favored the latter position. After three seasons, *Milenio* wrote with some satisfaction: "Jaime Camil has made *Jane the Virgin* into his family" (Moreno 2017). Here the Mexican star praises the "great union of the cast . . . in a foreign country" and claims it is a "privilege" simply to be a working actor in Los Angeles, much more so in a prestigious, prize-winning series like *Jane the Virgin*. He goes on: "It's a long journey . . . and *Jane the Virgin* doesn't portray Latinos as caricatures . . . saying 'fiesta' and 'tacos' and hanging piñatas from the ceiling."

Camil, through his pride in the show, thus attempts to inspire a similar emotion in his fellow countrypeople at a rare success abroad. Note that the Mexican actor does not mention here the "extreme storylines" considered typical of telenovelas and so closely associated with his character, plot points that showrunner Urman had identified as a key element in *Jane the Virgin*'s special appeal and tone. It is the realist, nonstereotypical elements that Camil prefers to highlight to his compatriots, whether they are skeptical or admiring.

Elsewhere, a rare interview with a first season writer celebrates "the Mexican woman who lends a Latin touch to *Jane the Virgin*" (Huerta Ortiz 2015b). Here, Carolina Rivera, a veteran of Mexican feature film and television who was interviewed back in Mexico, offers a different take on the series. Rivera claims that, at that time at least, she was the only Latin American writer in a pool of ten: "The writers' room is basically American Jews . . . and they're not familiar with Catholic rites, not even baptism or the *quinceañera*" (in "Chapter Eleven," Jane herself will briefly join the conflictive writers' room for Rogelio's *novela The Passions of Santos*). For the journalist, the Latin "humor and traditions" of the series (in which, we are helpfully told once more, "Jaime Camil acts") is thus thanks to the unique cultural contribution of this sole "Mexican writer." She is described, like Camil, as a migrant worker in Los Angeles, and one with valuable experience in telenovelas. It should be noted that by season three, Urman told *Hollywood Reporter* that she had "three Catholic writers" (Stanhope 2016). From season four, Rivera would be awarded a producer credit.

In a later interview, Camil stresses to *El Universal* (Monroy 2017) that although he was working in a prestigious American series, now in its third season, unlike some Mexicans in Hollywood he remained proud of his past experience in the serial melodrama at home. He is quoted as saying: "I have a fan base thanks to what I did in Mexico and Latin America, and I would be very ungrateful if I forgot it." Loyalty to Mexico is thus also loyalty to its national narrative of telenovelas. Although Camil clarifies here to the local audience that *Jane the Virgin* is a "series," not a *novela*, a certain continuity between the two genres and countries is confirmed. For example, Camil says that creator Jennie

Snyder Urman plans to include in the final season an homage to the seductive cross-dresser Camil played in one of his greatest successes in Mexican telenovela, *Por ella soy Eva* ("For Her, I'm Eva" [Televisa, 2012]) ("Jaime Camil seduce como Eva" 2017), a title that was being rerun in Mexico as late as 2024.

Nodding perhaps to the real-life origins of Jaime Camil, it is Mexico, not Venezuela, that has greater visibility at key moments in the show's decor, dialogue, and guest casting. For example, when Rogelio arranges a special lunch to impress his newly discovered daughter Jane in "Chapter Five," he has his studio crew rig up a backdrop of Chichén Itzá behind their dining table. Rogelio tells Jane that years ago he climbed the Mayan pyramid and prayed "for great fame."

Later, in "Chapter Twenty-Seven," in which Britney Spears guest stars, we learn that the two performers became friends after Rogelio was the first to wear the red vinyl catsuit that the singer borrowed for the music video for "Oops! . . . I Did It Again." The two friends broke up when, eager for publicity, he called the paparazzi on her as they were shopping together in Mexico City.

Rogelio's evil ex-wife and unwilling costar in the final episodes of *The Passions of Santos* is played by Kate del Castillo, in real life Mexico's most notorious telenovela lead ("Chapter Twenty-Eight"). Also in season two, Rogelio's treacherous assistant-cum-stalker Paola/Lola is created by recurring guest star Ana de la Reguera, one of the most acclaimed Mexican actresses in quality TV drama.

There is evidence that US audiences, more diverse than in Mexico, also responded well to Camil and his comic creation Rogelio. On *Jane the Virgin*'s subreddit, the Mexican actor elicits thoughtful posts by viewers who refer to their own varying command of the Spanish language ("r/JaneTheVirginCW"). OakTeach writes (spelling and punctuation have been preserved in all social media posts):

> Jaime Camil is I think the funniest person on this show . . . Some of the comedy is in JC's accented English, although it's

> not as pronounced as say Sofia Vergara's on Modern Family. But when he switches into speaking Spanish he goes from ham to heartthrob in a flash. He just seems so much more serious and competent . . . Does that happen for other viewers or is it just because I'm a Spanish speaker?

Commenters to this post reply variously that Camil is "hot as fire" in both languages; that "he is more mature-seeming . . . when he speaks Spanish (although I'm not a native speaker)"; and that "it is so refreshing to see a Spanish-speaking actor speak in English with a full on accent yet still with complete command and nuance of the English language."

This was the linguistic policy of showrunner Urman: that characters should speak both languages correctly at all times. Unlike in *Modern Family*, nonnative English never serves as a source of cheap humor, which might alienate the Latinx audience. Conversely, untranslated Swiss German is played for laughs in "Chapter Twenty-Six" of *Jane the Virgin* when yodelers pay an unlikely visit to the Marbella. In "Chapter Forty-One," Petra's long-lost twin from the Czech Republic, who is disastrously offered a waitress job at the Marbella, makes ridiculous mistakes involving English idioms (literally "hold[ing] the onions" at a customer's table) and grammar ("Why should I smile? I working"). The Spanish language, then, is a special case to be treated with proper respect.

More generally, the *Jane the Virgin* subreddit, founded on November 14, 2014, gives valuable evidence of the series' continuing audience years after it stopped broadcasting. The recap for the year 2023 (created on January 1, 2024) tells us that 180,440 people "visited this year"; that 143,808 "votes were cast" (for undemanding quizzes like "favorite scenes from the whole show"); that the top three posts include one on Jane's formal fashion choices (Rodriguez is pictured in full-length sapphire and emerald gowns); that the top three comments include one praising a "rare show where the 2 male leads [Michael and Rafael] were pretty great for the female lead"; that the three "most active countries" ("they love you over there") were the US, Canada, and the UK; and finally that there were 9,094 posts and comments, all adjudicated by just two hardworking and unpaid "mods" (moderators).

Coincidentally, fans focus on themes that I already cited in my introduction as central to this book, with the discussion of each topic handily accessible via Reddit's search function. There is a thread of posts on successive interviews with modest "anti-prestige showrunner" Jennie Snyder Urman; on the love triangle as central to the show's plot ("i HATE love triangles but *Jane the Virgin*'s is genuinely the best one i've ever seen"); on the "extreme differences" between the original telenovela *Juana la virgen* and the US series remake (a post written in English by an evidently fluent Spanish speaker); on the "Venezuelan lineage of the Villanuevas"; and on the depiction of immigration (the lengthy process followed by Jane's undocumented grandmother, Alba, mysterious to one viewer in the UK; a practical question as to how Alba can drive without papers).

In the show itself, this very serious topic will, typically, be sweetened by a humorous comment from Rogelio. Alba, comatose in a hospital bed after being thrown downstairs by Petra's mother, is threatened with the "medical repatriation" that on-screen titles reconfirm is a real thing. Rogelio reports: "I left word with the UN ambassador and [veteran singing star] Gloria Estefan. One of them will stop the deportation. Most probably Gloria Estefan" ("Chapter Ten"). In fact, it will be kindly police officer Michael who will make the call to the immigration authorities, even though he is at the time separated from Jane.

Finally, fans focus on LGBTQ+ issues, which raise unusually contradictory responses. One poster praises "lesbian connections" in the show. Another celebrates the "magnificent queering" of the romper-wearing Petra, initially Rafael's neglected, spiteful wife, later to take a female lawyer as her lover. Conversely, a third complains about "homophobia in the writing," and a fourth asks why "all the villains" on the show are queer. Yet antagonists like the flame-haired lesbian Rose, the irrepressible mother-in-law of Rafael and the enduring lover of his sister, are as glamorous and seductive as they are evil.

The *Jane the Virgin* subreddit rules, prominently pinned to the top of the site and revised on January 1, 2013, are also revelatory of a kind and supportive community that aims to reproduce the positive values of the "warm-hearted" series and is "excited to see NEW viewers are still discovering" the show. The first rule is "No Spoilers in Post Titles," pointing to the fact that new Netflix viewers are still watching the series in traditional broadcast style, sequentially from beginning to end. The definition of spoilers reveals fans' main plot priorities, whose secrets must be jealously guarded until the final, hundredth episode: "who lives or dies"; "who Jane ends up with"; "who the Narrator is." The second rule is "Be Respectful" ("people are allowed to disagree but no[t] to treat each other badly"), and the third is "Redundant Posts May Be Removed."

Once more, the definition of such posts shows what fans take for granted and do not need to be reminded of. Under this category, as expected, comes the allegiance to dueling love rivals via "Team Michael" or "Team Rafael" (playfully addressing such fan culture, in "Chapter Seventeen" Rogelio will declare himself in all caps #TEAMMICHAEL, complete with on-screen hashtag). However, in addition and more surprisingly, comes the question "DAE [does anyone else] hate Jane?" In spite of Gina Rodriguez's prominence in the US press and in the series, then, some fans post that they watch her show for the supporting characters, like villainous, mysterious Petra or cheesy, cheeky Rogelio.

The other main fan resource, the flamingo-pink-hued *Jane the Virgin* wiki, is now less active than the subreddit, although it is admirably polyglot, boasting smaller versions in Spanish and French (no doubt to the disappointment of Filipino fans, whom Rodriguez took the trouble to visit in their home country at one point, a promised site in Tagalog does not in fact seem to exist) ("Jane the Virgin"). Posts on the

441 pages of the English-language wiki tend to focus on themes considered redundant on subreddit, such as the love triangle. Yet even here fans sometimes reveal a thoughtful engagement with the series and a self-conscious awareness of the differences between television fiction and the real world. For example, Tepsu writes at length on July 23, 2020, controversially claiming, "I'm team Michael and team Rafael" and asking, "why do we have to choose one of them and hate the other?" The user testifies to intense emotion over a tragic plot point when romantic, reliable Michael apparently dies (he returns transformed in the final season): "I was heartbroken. It was the most I cried over a tv show ever." Yet they conclude: "In real life you want a relationship like Jane and Michael. But in a tv show Jane and Rafael are perfect. They have drama and chemistry."

The rest of the wiki testifies to this dual focus of unabashed emotion on the one hand (of fans' affection for their favorite characters and romances) and disinterested analysis on the other (of fans' commentary on production processes and narrative structure). Stressing the latter, the home page hosts four extended videos, two of which show the showrunner and main cast at formal television industry events: the Paley Fest (media museum) in Los Angeles 2015 and the Screen Actors Guild–American Federation of Television and Radio Artists (SAG-AFTRA, an actor trade union foundation) in 2017. A third shows cast member Justin Baldoni as his thoughtful actor self, not as his playboy character Rafael, discussing "Why I'm done trying to be 'man enough.'" A subpage called "Backstage" gives full professional biographies of cast and crew.

Even when the wiki limits itself to exploring the fictional world of the series, it does so in a way that fleshes out our understanding of the show's story space—in a way that might be called "scholarly." For example, a detailed timeline begins back in February 1946 with the birth of Mateo, Jane's long dead grandfather, who appears in a flashback in "Chapter Twenty-Five," and extends to May 2021, when his widow Alba gains US citizenship. Other subpages document the series' varied locations, even including the "expensive house" (secretly paid for by Petra) to which Jane and Michael move briefly in season three; and the many faux telenovelas cited in the show, from the science fiction *This Is Mars* (the image shows Rogelio on the deck of a clone of the Starship Enterprise) to the historical romance *Fernando e Isabel* (the image shows Rogelio's archrival and nemesis, Esteban Santiago, in period garb).

Prominently quoting on its masthead Rogelio's advice to Jane in moments of crisis—"Inhala. Exhala"—the wiki invites viewers to breathe deeply and contemplate the full extent of Jane Gloriana Villanueva's universe. It is a world to which faithful fans continue to contribute even after the production team has moved on, and viewers' creative contributions are ironically but warmly referenced within the show itself. In "Chapter Twenty-Six," Rogelio proudly shows the bemused Xiomara a marionette of himself, complete with lavender uniform, that he keeps in his dressing room. His explanation? "It's fan art."

INTERMISSION 2
THE FIRST SEASON FINALE ("CHAPTER TWENTY-TWO")

Michael, Jane, and Rafael at the hospital after the Braxton-Hicks contractions.

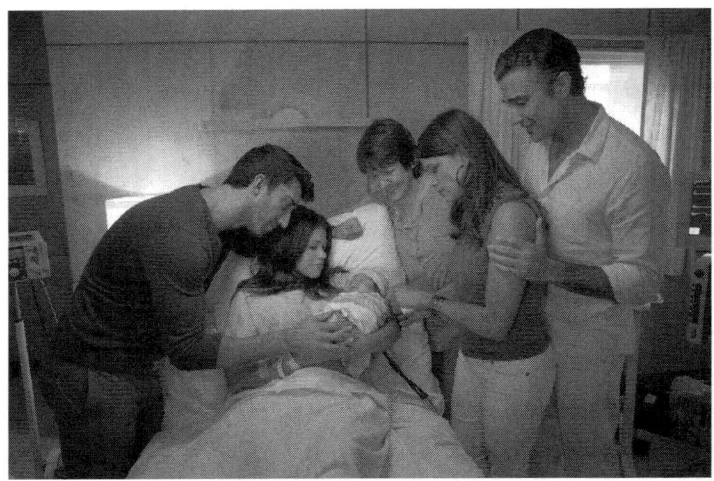

From left: The baby's father Rafael, Jane, baby Mateo, great-grandmother Alba, grandmother Xiomara, and grandfather Rogelio after the birth.

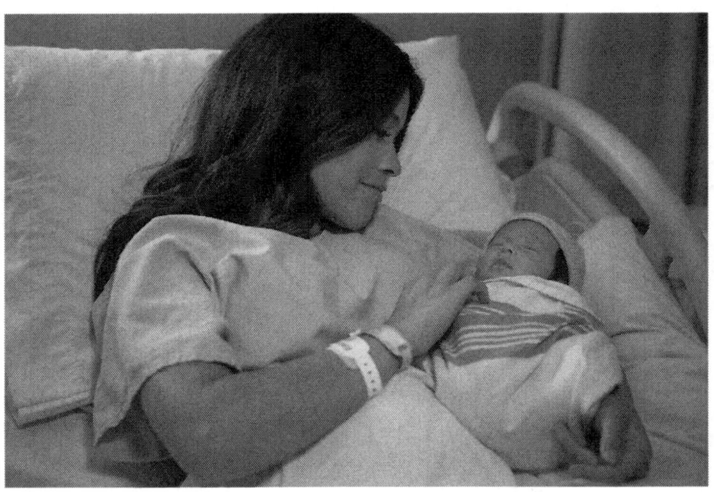

Jane and Mateo, virgin and child.

The twenty-second episode of the inaugural season of *Jane the Virgin* (referred to as ever as a "chapter") aired on May 11, 2015, nearly seven months after the pilot episode premiered. Inside the series, nine months have passed, from Jane's insemination to her giving birth. Despite the show's eventual ratings success, The CW, as a minor network, had reason to believe that the unique narrative of the series was not initially clear. As a result, the forty-two-minute episode (which was rounded up to the traditional hour with commercial breaks) employed various techniques to engage the audience, mindful of the limitations of this old-style broadcast series. Unlike Netflix viewers, who can easily revisit previous episodes, at least for as long as the streaming service retains the rights to the show, traditional TV viewers could not do so without taking the trouble to record and save past episodes on their DVRs.

One of the key techniques used in the season one finale is of course the anonymous and omniscient Spanish-accented Narrator, known as the "Latin Lover" in Netflix's subtitles. In this finale he provides a rapid recap of the entire first season in the opening minutes, directly addressing the audience, invoking their connection with the main character, and giving her full name, Jane Gloriana Villanueva. The Narrator playfully references the show's melodrama-inspired nature, asking here as so often elsewhere, "Straight out of a telenovela, right?"

The precredits sequence engages the audience by offering additional backstory for the new episode (opening flashbacks are very common in episodes of the series). This includes a glimpse into Jane's birth twenty-four years earlier and the wise advice of her grandmother, Alba, at that time, delivered in Spanish: "Cinco minutos de dolor por una vida entera de felicidad" (translated as "Five minutes of pain for a lifetime of happiness" in the subtitles). This moment exemplifies the series' positive depictions of Latina characters and the portrayal of female genealogy over generations and across languages. Here, as ever, the Villanueva women are bilingual, understanding both Spanish and English, whichever language is being spoken at the time, and all characters pronounce Spanish names correctly (although only Rogelio says "Marbella" right, as in the name of the luxury beach resort in Spain). This biculturalism is reinforced in the opening credits, which continue to acknowledge both major American studios, Warner Bros and CBS, and the lesser-known Venezuelan network and production company RCTV, the original source. As we shall see in the third chapter, RCTV had ceased operations in Venezuela due to political reasons, reflecting the show's inevitable connection to real-world events.

The first present-day sequence of the finale highlights the easy camaraderie and intimacy among the female characters. In the family kitchen, the heavily pregnant Jane pretends to experience contractions to play a prank on her mother, Xiomara, while making her perennial favorite, grilled cheese sandwiches. The scene emphasizes the strong bond among the women in the Villanueva family and the absence of significant male contributions or support at this key point in the story (Jane has by now broken up with both of her suitors). The editing employs quick cuts to advance the plot and highlight now-familiar key themes common to the series and its telenovela prototype, such as cross-class romance and the love triangle. Then comes a conversation between Rafael and his sister Luisa about Jane. Petra, Rafael's now estranged wife, unexpectedly interrupts the moment with a phone call, leading to another recap, this time of her outrageous behavior over the entire season. The audience witnesses the different perspectives of the same scene through Rafael and Jane's perspectives, revealing their contrasting views on the situation.

This episode also focuses on Rogelio. He is portrayed, as ever, as a self-obsessed but endearing character, emphasizing the show's blend of humor and drama. Rogelio's new enthusiasm is for what he calls the "cultural Mecca" of Las Vegas, where he hopes to star in a revival of the musical *Jesus Christ Superstar* (in "Chapter Twelve" Rogelio was fired from *The Passions of Santos* due to the scheming of his evil assistant). Rogelio's elaborate plans for the Vegas visit with Jane's mother, where Rogelio will star in what he calls a "residency" of just one night, contribute to the episode's comedic tone.

Meanwhile, the contrast between Jane and Petra remains notable in terms of appearance and character. Jane, portrayed by Gina Rodriguez, favors a simple, natural look and a modest hairstyle that she has retained throughout her pregnancy (her maternal wear is, however, varied and aesthetic over the course of this first season). In contrast, Yael Grobglas's Czech immigrant Petra embodies a different image with her carefully styled blond hair, tall, slender frame, and meticulous appearance (in the previous episode, Petra's pink sweater carefully matched her lipstick and her turquoise necklace complemented her eyes). This contrast highlights the show's commitment to challenging beauty standards that were once near ubiquitous on American television. The series thus continues to depict its version of Miami as a diverse and inclusive world, and it features a cast that emphasizes the show's connections both to the Latinx community and the broader cultural landscape beyond it, such as the presence of Eastern European immigrants.

The plot in this special episode features parallel storylines involving two couples, (the broken up) Rafael and ex-wife Petra, and (the also broken up) Jane and her former fiancé, Michael. Both couples are nonetheless arranging dinner dates that will be disrupted by the unexpected birth of Jane's child. These scenes play on traditional telenovela themes of sentimental romance. Conversely, the birth of Jane's child in the hospital, after yet another comic bus trip, is a climactic moment in the whole series and is marked by wholly serious performances. The camera even captures this moment subjectively, highlighting Jane's epidural-related gaps in consciousness by rare fades to white (the same technique will be used in the parallel sequence where Petra gives birth, accompanied only by Jane, in "Chapter Thirty-Six"). Confirming her fidelity to family, Jane will finally name her baby Mateo, after the maternal grandfather she never knew.

The episode concludes with a series of more farcical or melodramatic cliff-hangers, including a revelation about Xiomara and Rogelio's drunken Vegas wedding (which is a surprise even to them), the discovery of another vial of Rafael's sperm (by villainess Petra), and the dramatic abduction of Jane's newborn child by the mysterious drug kingpin known as Sin Rostro ("Faceless"), who has by now been identified as Rose ("Sin Rose-tro" puns an on-screen title). Rose, who buried her wealthy husband in wet concrete in "Chapter Twelve," is, we will recall, the former lover (and stepmother) of Rafael's doctor sister. These cliff-hangers serve to bridge the first season and the upcoming second season, engaging viewers with a mix of comedy, drama, and telenovela elements. The finale also demonstrates an attempt to embrace intermediality, as it encourages viewers to engage with the show on social media through on-screen hashtags. This use of hashtags during the broadcast reflects a contemporary approach to actively collaborating with the audience in an era before on-demand streaming.

Despite the episode's focus on the birth and the drama that ensues, this finale somewhat neglects the broader Latinx issues, such as immigration and access to health care, that were important to the show's audience, as Jane's hospital stay is presented as a nonissue. The conclusion of the season finale highlights rather the familial connections and traditions within the Latinx community, as the three generations of women gather in the hospital, repeating a message of pain and joy across the decades.

Rafael's evolving character and his new commitment to fatherhood also challenge traditional notions of masculinity (as will actor Justin Baldoni outside the show). Michael, too, is finally sensitive and respectful, even though the two rivalrous suitors fought earlier in the episode when Jane was hospitalized with Braxton-Hicks contractions. Ultimately, the first season finale's function is to set the stage for the series' second season, leaving viewers eager to see how the various cliff-hangers and evolving character dynamics will be resolved in the next installment.

There is no doubt that this first season finale was successful in fulfilling this aim, and you can still trace the televisual history of this episode and relive fans' experience by conducting a search for the Twitter (now X) hashtag that was displayed on-screen during the original broadcast: #JanesHavingABaby. This hashtag continues to appear in posts dated not only to the night of the broadcast but also in the extensive digital trail that followed. The show's creator @JennieUrman expressed her excitement for the #JanetheVirgin finale just before the 9:00 p.m. screening on May 11, 2015, addressing the audience with genuine enthusiasm and just a touch of irony: "I can't stand it. Seriously." Subsequently, fans began emphasizing the themes already mentioned in my close reading above, particularly the idea of solidarity. For example, the day after the broadcast, one fan posted beneath an image of the three generations at the birth, stating that the Villanueva women were always together (@Baedoniunite, May 12, 2015). On the night of the finale, other audience members shared their mixed emotions and the challenges of watching linear TV at the time. One viewer complained about the weather report interrupting the #JanetheVirginfinale and wondered what Jane's mother said to the bus driver on the way to the hospital (@kebert2thumbsup, May 11, 2015).

The intense on-screen emotions of the characters were mirrored off-screen, both at the time and during subsequent viewings, as fans narrated their joy and tears over the show's events. For instance, one tweeter hoped that baby Mateo would bring Jane and Rafael back together (@latinjc4u, May 11, 2015). Another fan, a full three years later, on March 13, 2018, described the experience of rewatching *Jane the Virgin* and still not being able to stop crying, finding the birth scene so beautiful (@ElizabethArme14).

A dedicated superfan from Michigan later offered an extensive thread of ten thoughtful tweets on the finale, praising Jane's courage during her graduate school interview; citing Rogelio's unconsciously humorous quips (when he abandons the Las Vegas theater for the Miami hospital: "There are many Jesus Christs. There is only one Jane"); admiring her favorite Villanueva women and their amazement at the newborn being a boy (hitherto, they had only given birth to girls); and celebrating the first season finale as the wildest thing she had ever seen, while anticipating the equally wild finales of future seasons of the show (@ashleymmaynard, May 1, 2019).

Beyond the discussions on the dedicated subreddit and wiki that I mentioned before, Twitter was the main platform for US TV fan discussions at the time. It is perhaps no accident that the microblogging site is repeatedly referenced in the show itself, as when Rogelio is highly concerned that he is losing followers due to the retweeting of a ridiculous GIF that shows him mishandling his space gun on *Pasión intergaláctica* ("Chapter Sixteen"). It is also clear that viewers who posted on Twitter for the season finale were more focused on feminist rather than Latinx issues. Many viewers shared the intense emotions they felt with this welcoming fan community, while others, more ambitiously, engaged in creative speculation about upcoming plot twists. One even suggested that the off-screen Narrator might turn out to be Jane's grown son Mateo, whose birth the audience had just witnessed (@deepsoap, May 12, 2015). We will see later whether this turned out to be the case.

2
TEXT AND CONTEXT

This chapter delves into the intricate narrative structure of the series across its five seasons (*Variety* expressed early doubts about how the show could consistently "churn out such twists" [Lowry 2014]). The initial, familiar storylines of cross-class romance and a love triangle quickly expand into unexpected territory such as police procedural, involving shockingly sudden changes in tone. One minor character will meet his death at a fancy party at the Marbella, impaled on an ice sculpture of a marlin ("Marlin, not Merlin!" insists Petra) as early as "Chapter Two." There is little doubt that the enigmatic master criminal Sin Rostro is to blame.

My own second chapter also explores how this wide-ranging narrative intersects with the social and political themes that are crucial to the diverse appeal of *Jane the Virgin*. These themes encompass not only feminist and Latinx issues but also queer elements, with prominent lesbian characters in a genre that is normally centered on heterosexual romance. You will recall that Luisa, the doctor who accidentally inseminates Jane, is the lesbian sister of sperm donor Rafael. Luisa, who once loved red-haired Rose, Luisa and Rafael's stepmother, will start a new romance in season two with Michael's new partner, Susanna, or so she believes (this will also work out very badly).

The rapid pace of Jane's life introduces some surprises in the course of the first season. At one point, she will opt for Rafael shortly before her wedding to faithful fiancé Michael is meant to take place. Jane will cycle between the two, and other boyfriends, thereafter. The second and third seasons bring significant new challenges, from raising a baby as a single mother to navigating long-delayed marriage and sexual experience. The word "virgin" in the title will henceforward be crossed out and substituted by a succession of other qualifiers (including "widow"). As Jane attempts to realize her challenging dream of becoming a writer ("Be brave!"), the show delves into young women's halting but determined professional aspirations and how they intersect with personal plans. However, the unique narrative technique of the omniscient voice-over in *Jane the Virgin*, breaking the fourth wall as it does, complicates the social implications of these serious but unpreachy themes with its jaunty commentary on the series' action.

At certain points, Jane explicitly mentions that her "timeline" has been disrupted by insemination, pregnancy, and motherhood. However, as the series progresses, its concept of temporality extends beyond this linear storytelling with flashbacks to the past and future twists. *Jane the Virgin*'s commitment to portraying positive images ensures that every member of a diverse cast is presented with dignity at some point in their intricate storylines. Rafael's ruthless wife Petra, whose real name is revealed in season two as Natalia, endured hardships on her journey from Eastern Europe's poverty and violence to a wealthy lifestyle in Florida. She is also burdened with caring for her unsympathetic mother, who has shared her odyssey. In later seasons she will be gifted by the writers with both picture-perfect twins and a touching lesbian affair. Yet as late as "Chapter Thirty-Four" she will still tell Jane, with unselfconscious malice: "I do feel better knowing that you suffered a little."

While the plot may appear complex on paper, one of the publicity posters for the first season simplifies the initial concept when translated into a visual format. Its humorously bathetic tagline reads: "Passion. Deception. Corruption. Insemination." In the center, a smilingly complicit Jane, wearing a shocking pink lacey dress, is haloed by the radiant Miami sun. Standing closest behind her, on the right and left,

The poster for the first season.

are her competing suitors, Rafael and Michael. Behind them are the key family members: Jane's mother Xiomara and grandmother Alba. In the final row, you find more distant characters in the drama: Jane's long-absent father, Rogelio, and Rafael's cunning wife, Petra. The Florida setting is referenced by stylized palm tree fronds, underscoring the heightened backdrop shared by the seven central characters.

A parallel promotional image for the second season features the same cast but in a different setting and with a different emphasis. Now the scene is at the beach. Jane sits in the center on a folding chair wearing a round sun hat that suggests a halo once more. Now, however, she is holding baby Mateo on her lap (attentive spectators can make out the slogan on the child's T-shirt: "My mom is a virgin"). Behind her stand a sober Rafael, the child's biological father, and a grinning Rogelio, the maternal grandfather, holding what appear to be tiny beach balls. Jane is flanked on the sand by her own smiling mother and grandmother, while on the margins a seductive Petra lolls in high heels (on the beach!) and boy-next-door police officer Michael, clad in more sensible shoes, smiles winningly at the spectator over to the other side. Such promotional posters serve to remind forgetful viewers of the principal cast, but they also hint at changing narrative priorities. Michael, marginalized in the image, will be subject to a shocking cliff-hanger at the end of the second season. Moreover, the fact that Petra sports a round sun hat like Jane's, albeit bigger and pinker, suggests a possible rapprochement between these two bitter rivals.

Even after its first season ended there was some confusion in the TV industry as to *Jane the Virgin*'s hybrid genre. On March 17, 2015, *Variety* wrote that the series "would be considered a comedy" at the Emmy awards even though its hour-long length classified it as a drama (comedies were normally restricted to episodes of thirty minutes) (Birnbaum 2015). As different genres involve different conventions and expectations, *Jane the Virgin*'s tragicomic tone made it potentially troublesome. The series would be controversially shut out of the Emmys, with a nomination going only to the voice acting of the Narrator by Anthony

The poster for the second season.

Mendez. The revelation of the identity of Latin Lover, long guessed by fans, would be one of the several mysteries solved in the final episode.

A test case here, for what is often called by fond fans their "comfort show," was the decision in "Chapter Fifty-Four" to kill off Michael, by now Jane's husband and a longtime favorite of his vociferous "team" of shippers. Michael had survived an earlier shooting twenty episodes before but suddenly succumbed to an aortic dissection from his wound. When showrunner Jennie Snyder Urman was interviewed on this "shocking twist" by *Hollywood Reporter* on February 6, 2017, she made clear that it had been long planned in her show's plotting: It was "just part of the larger arc" (Stanhope 2017). Urman notes that as early as "Chapter Ten" she had given this ominous line to the Narrator: "Michael would love Jane as long as he lived, until he drew his very last breath." Likewise, the creator says that there would be rare "dramatic, life-changing events" in the show, comparing Jane's insemination at the start of the series to Michael's death here "at the mid-point."

Urman's concern for the viewers' feelings is shown by her open letter on microblogging website Tumblr, which is addressed to "Dearest Jane Fans" ("Jane the Virgin" *Tumblr*). Here Urman cites the premonitions of a beloved character's fate; praises the "magic" of actor Brett

Dier; and reassures viewers that he and his character will not be forgotten: "Michael will be missed in Jane's world, just as Brett is already missed in ours." Urman's letter demonstrates the dueling demands of fiction and reality that we have seen in fan forums online. Elsewhere, in the show itself, mourning is characteristically undercut by comedy. As the cast exits a funeral in "Chapter Fourteen," Rogelio opines of his own presence: "On such sad days it helps people to see a celebrity."

When the whole series ended two years later, Urman confirmed that its main story arc had been plotted across an anticipated five seasons from the very start: "I could figure out how many swerves along the road before you got to the final destination" (Bentley 2019). The satisfied creator here invokes telenovela with its happy ending, often a wedding, one last time. Rogelio's *The Passions of Santos*, the first cheesy show within the show, will likewise end with a dramatized white wedding, complete with rainbow backdrop ("Chapter Twenty-Eight"). His nonfictional wedding with longtime partner Xiomara, during a hurricane no less, will serve as the dramatic finale to season three. Urman evidently knows that the difference between the two genres is that a telenovela always comes to this kind of definitive conclusion, while a US network series at the mercy of its ratings may arrive at an inconclusive ending after an indefinite number of seasons. Here, once more, *Jane the Virgin* is unique in building to the satisfying ending of a chronicle that was long foretold.

Beyond the prefiguring of the conclusion, deep structuring devices work through and across the seasons, punctuated by shocking cliff-hangers, such as the kidnapping of a newborn child or a shooting on a wedding night. (Satirizing itself, the series ends "Chapter Twenty-Five" with a literal cliff-hanger: Rogelio holds tight to a cardboard rock on his flagrantly artificial studio set, while balancing on a stepladder just out of shot.) The first of the main structuring devices is the love triangle, which enables willing fans to join competing "teams" (this does not appear in the Venezuelan original). The second is the cross-class romance, which adds a realist touch to the fantasy (this does appear in *Juana la virgen*, where the contrast between rich and poor families is yet more marked than in *Jane the Virgin*).

Outside the three points of the main triangle, subsidiary relationships offer support in carefully crafted subplots. They are helpfully set out by the wiki's "Romances" page ("Jane the Virgin" *Fandom*). Jane herself is given two post-Michael flings: clueless, shirtless telenovela actor Fabian (daytime soap star Francisco San Martin) in season three; and tattooed, hipster comic book artist Adam (*Teen Wolf* star Tyler Posey) in season four. Petra's deeply felt lesbian affair with her lawyer JR ("She broke up with me and I feel like someone cut out a piece of my heart" ["Chapter Ninety-One"]) extends over eighteen episodes and several murders in seasons four and five. Rogelio and Xiomara ("Ro and Xo") may be each other's true loves, despite the decades-long gap in which they did not see each other. However, longing for the second child whom Xiomara chooses not to give him, Rogelio enters into a coparenting agreement in season three with feisty matchmaker Darci (Justina Machado). She says they are just perfect together: "Two aging narcissists" ("Chapter Fifty-One").

As can be seen above, unexpected plot points intersect with surprising character arcs. The unmaternal Petra proves to be more sympathetic than at the start when she plans to blackmail Rafael with his sperm so he will remain in a loveless marriage. In the second season, she will self-inseminate herself with Rafael's newly discovered second semen sample and thus move into single motherhood, a position originally occupied by Jane (still, Petra relies on a troupe of nannies). Rogelio grows less egotistical than in the opening episodes. One of my favorite early moments is in "Chapter Three" when, asked for a signature at a hotel check-in, Rogelio assumes that the unwitting clerk is requesting his autograph: "Who shall I make it out to?" Soon Rogelio will show his commitment to the Xiomara he had abandoned twenty-three years before. He will also struggle, like Jane, to reconcile his personal responsibilities as a member of a new family with his professional priorities as a transnational TV actor, which are slyly satirized by the series. Another favorite Rogelio moment comes in "Chapter Sixteen" when he professes: "I take my craft very seriously. Which you can see by my use of the word 'craft.'"

The most ambiguous and ubiquitous structuring device in the series is the off-screen Narrator, with his arch catchphrases ("It should be noted . . ."; "You will recall . . .") and hints, even at the most dramatic moments, that he may be "unreliable" ("Chapter Fifty-Four"). Although Latin Lover bears much of the burden of campy comedy in *Jane the Virgin*, even competing with a rival female narrator in the season four premiere, the device is in fact infrequent in Latin American telenovelas. One exception at the time of writing is the *Vencer* ["Overcoming"] franchise (TelevisaUnivision, 2020–present), the highest rated in Mexico this decade. In *Vencer*, a key character in one season, such as a feminist journalist, becomes a narrator in the next, informing the audience in Mexico about such questions as the dangers of intimate exposure on social media. The status of *Jane the Virgin*'s anonymous Narrator is more ambiguous. From the start, his presence raises questions of authorship, complicating the plot and making us wonder whose story we are watching. Is it Jane's, the protagonist of the drama, or Latin Lover's, whose spoken comments consistently interrupt and interpret the drama?

In "Chapter Fifty-Seven," Jane loses her voice and regains it, literally and metaphorically, only when she goes back to working on her first novel, a version of her love story with Michael in the form of a historical romance. We see sepia-tinted sequences recreated by the regular cast in period costume in the show itself. Titled *Snow Falling*, the novel appeared in real life in 2017 with extravagantly romantic cover art and lightly changed names (Rafael becomes "Rake"). Given the steamy Florida setting, the "snow" of the title is, as in the show once more, plaster falling from a ceiling or white blossoms from a tree. Faithful to its fictional origin, the author's name is given on the front as "Jane Gloriana Villanueva," and the work of the ghostwriter, Caridad Piñeiro, is confined to a gag on the back cover: "So much fun I wish I'd written it myself!" As Piñeiro noted in an interview, the connection with the series, including the inclusion of commentary by the

Narrator set in italics, is respectful of the TV audience's deep investment in the original story (Walker 2017). Proof of the novel's relevance to fans, on the publication of the book, entertainment news site *Vulture* published "10 Things You Learn from the *Jane the Virgin* Book *Snow Falling*" (VanArendonk 2017).

Beyond these formal devices and transmedia extensions of *Jane the Virgin*'s universe, recurrent themes knit the series together, over five lengthy seasons and one hundred smart, frantic, and emotional episodes. First comes feminism. The reconciliation of the personal and professional, urgent in the case of single motherhood, is arguably the most vital in the whole show. Jane may frequently change her romantic partners, but she is always loyal to her much-frustrated goal of becoming a published writer. In "Chapter Fifteen," inspired by the presence of her favorite novelist, Angelique Harper, at the Marbella, we see Jane magically transformed into a tousle-haired Victorian heroine herself as she pounds on her computer keyboard. In this sequence her name is changed, significantly perhaps, to "Juana," the same name as the protagonist of the original Venezuelan *novela*.

Typically (humorously) Rogelio gets the wrong end of the stick about feminism, a topic that Jane takes seriously. In "Chapter Seventeen," he offers to treat Michael to a "mani-pedi." When the police officer protests, Rogelio replies: "It's 2015. Men get pedicures. Or what was all this 'equal rights' talk about?" Or again in "Chapter Thirty-Four," when working on his time-travel telenovela, Rogelio mansplains to Xiomara: "I'm playing the nation's first male feminist. I think history has really overlooked his point of view." The hashtag #firstmalefeminist helpfully appears on-screen. The writers even have Rogelio say to his coparent Darci before politely requesting a kiss: "Donald Trump has ruined romance for all of us" ("Chapter Fifty-Three"). Conversely, in "Chapter Thirty-Seven," Jane's feminist thesis adviser gives a succinct response to her student's attempt at romantic fiction: "Barf."

Reproductive health care is also a constant, although it is treated in different ways at different times and for different characters. Jane rejects the possibility of abortion that was offered by her mother in "Chapter One," but in "Chapter Fifteen," when her mother fears she is pregnant after not taking her contraceptive pill, Jane will criticize her harshly: "I had an accident. You were reckless." In "Chapter Twenty-Five," the scheming Petra, who has fallen pregnant after self-insemination, considers three alternatives: coparenting the child (actually twins) with Rafael, getting an abortion, or telling a random Russian oligarch that he is the father. Finally, in "Chapter Forty-Six," Xiomara will reveal that she chose to abort an unplanned child fathered by Rogelio's rival Esteban, a decision the showrunner insists is not "tortured" (Stanhope 2016). Before Xiomara and her crucifix-wearing mother are reconciled, however, there is a heartfelt discussion between them.

One scholar finds a surprising source for *Jane the Virgin*'s plotting in the female-penned "sentimental novel" of the early nineteenth century. For Natalie Rose, *Jane the Virgin* "updates" melodramatic tropes, such as unwed motherhood, which have a lengthy heritage in US mass fiction (Rose 2019). In the college class that Jane teaches, she will cite Jane Austen on the pleasures and perils of matrimony ("Chapter Thirty-One"). The reference to the British author will recur in the novel *Snow Falling*, where heroine Josephine attends readings of Austen at her public library (Villanueva 2017, 104). But maternity is also shown to change with the times. In "Chapter Seventeen," grandmother, mother, and daughter argue bitterly about different styles of parenting. Also, the pregnant Jane is perplexed by the requirements of modern motherhood: the swaddling, the lactation class, the doula, and the "baby wrap" (which, her friend Lina says helpfully, enables the mother to wear a child "like an accessory"). She also debates whether to join the online community "Milky Madres."

The Latinx question has also attracted attention. For example, academics ask to what extent the immigration process of Jane's abuela is accurate as depicted in the series, and they question whether the fluent bilingualism typical of Jane's household corresponds to real life. First, then, in "Alba the Undocumented: Immigration Law and

Citizenship Excess in *Jane the Virgin*," Litzy Galarza praises the series as the only one to have "illustrated the three juridical status changes required to complete an undocumented immigrant's journey to naturalized citizenship" (Galarza 2022). This plotline for Jane's grandmother serves as "public pedagogy for understanding the role of immigration law in society." We might add that this pedagogy is also emotional. Alba will receive her longed-for green card at Christmas, and it will be placed in a position of honor with the angel tree topper that her now-dead husband crafted so many years before ("Chapter Thirty-One"). Her citizenship ceremony will be one of many dramatic high points in a frantic season four finale.

Secondly, in "'Oh, I Don't Even Know How to Say This in Spanish': The Linguistic Representation of Latinxs in *Jane the Virgin*," Victoria Melgarejo and Mary Bucholtz praise the unstereotypical "believable characters and linguistic dynamics" in the series (Melgarejo and Bucholtz 2020). Such dynamics include an "intergenerational language shift" (Alba speaks perfect Spanish, Jane perfect English), linguistic accommodation (Rogelio, uniquely, switches languages according to his addressee), and code-switching (the hybrid Spanglish that is in fact almost never heard in the show). The sociolinguists suggest that *Jane the Virgin* "diverges from real-world Latinx language use," as in practice grandparents and grandchildren may find communication difficult. However, the series will nonetheless "be perceived as authentic" by Latinx and Anglo viewers alike.

The progress made by *Jane the Virgin* on the earlier pioneer *Ugly Betty* should be noted. When Betty, exceptionally, speaks Spanish, the humor derives from her misuse of false cognates, as when she says she is "embarazada" (Spanish for "pregnant," not "embarrassed"). *Jane the Virgin*'s characters never make such clownish linguistic errors. Indeed, when courteous Rogelio first meets Alba, he modifies his Spanish catchphrase to address the breathless older woman with proper respect: "Inhala. Exhala" becomes "Inhale. Exhale." Alba's own first sentence in English takes the form of a complex conditional sentence, beginning: "If this did not happen . . ." ("Chapter Twenty"). And *Jane the Virgin* does not shy away from linguistic controversy. In "Chapter Sixty-One," an Anglo customer tells a Spanish speaker in the Marbella gift shop: "This is America. You should learn how to speak English." Alba feels ashamed that she was not brave enough to speak back to the woman in defense of her native language, but she will make her own first lengthy speech in English at the party after her citizenship ceremony ("Chapter Eighty-One").

Finally, queer issues offer a throughline over the seasons. Lesbian characters are unusually prominent, from the harassed doctor Luisa in "Chapter One," who will prove admirably proactive, if unlucky and deluded, in her sex life, to Petra's affair with JR, whom she meets in "Chapter Seventy-Two" and, to her great surprise, falls in love with. Gay men are less prominent, but Rogelio, who brags that he appeared on the cover of *Out* magazine, throws a "big gay dinner" for his parents after his father comes out of the closet in order to show how gay-friendly he is ("Chapter Thirty-One"). The hashtag #LOVEWINS appears on-screen in rainbow-colored letters.

Once more there is some ambivalence here. When Adam, Jane's boyfriend in season four, comes out as bisexual in "Chapter Sixty-Nine" (he is played by openly queer and gender-fluid actor Tyler Posey [Tabberer 2021]), "Jane the heteronormative" is initially concerned by his same-sex relationships. Still, by the end of the episode she tries out a kiss herself with best friend Lina. Speculation as to whether the Narrator is gay or not is encouraged by carefully placed hints in his monologue. Back on the subreddit, lesbian viewers celebrate their fantasy passion for Jane, even as they acknowledge the real-life inaccessibility of the actress who plays her. One typical post, under a picture of the star tousle-haired on a beach chair, reads: "Gina Rodriguez appreciation: I wish she was single. And gay. And not out of my league" (@basilfetish 2020).

Jane the Virgin depicts LGBTQ+ citizens as ubiquitous and autonomous, living their own lives without apology in the series' rainbow-hued version of the tropical metropolis of Miami. It also takes for granted that independent women should have control over their reproductive health and Latinx people may negotiate immigration and linguistic dynamics as they think fit. Compare how Anthony Mendez (the voice of "Latin Lover," who works out of his home studio in New Jersey) put it to *The New York Times* on his Emmy nomination: "We [Latinos] are as American as anyone else, and we can cross over just by speaking the way we speak normally" (Shattuck 2015). *Jane the Virgin* thus "normalizes" all kinds of people, making them "just as American as anyone else," even as it works so hard to preserve and respect their delightful and ever-surprising idiosyncrasy.

In the middle of writing this book, I reached out to fans on the subreddit. On January 3, 2024, I asked them what they loved about the series; how they first discovered it; and how they were coping now that there were no new episodes. Reddit had allotted me the username Cute-Satisfaction827 and the avatar of an old-style TV set like the one the Villanuevas watch. Three of the responses, all posted just two days later, proved especially thoughtful and sensitive. They also showed how plotlines, characters, and social issues, the subjects of this chapter, interact with the pure pleasure of watching your comfort show.

Affectionate_Cow_579 focuses on the romantic side of *Jane the Virgin*. They start the post with a quote from Angelique Harper, a romance writer who is a character in the show: "The night whispered with promise." They say the sentence "sums up the whole series." Although they are Team Rafael, they praise Jane's kisses with both suitors, showing a keen awareness of the setting: the first is under a tree with snow-like blossoms falling outside the Marbella, the second in front of a papier-mâché mountain with fake snow falling inside the Marbella. Although they are no fan of Jane's mother Xiomara, they love the "Xo/Ro" relationship because Rogelio is "so sweet and funny and earnest." They also appreciate the surprising arc of Jane's relationship with Petra over the seasons, from enemies to "reluctant friends" to something like "sisters." Affectionate_Cow_579 also carefully curates comic episodes, calling attention to Gina Rodriguez's physical humor, even during her emotional, single-take monologue when Michael comes back from the dead. I return to this tour de force in my fourth Intermission, which is devoted to "Chapter Eighty-Two."

Tall-Move6136's take is different. They show how accidental a future superfan's path to the series can be, writing that even though they "grew up watching novelas," when *Jane the Virgin* was being promoted in 2014, "I thought . . . the concept was going to be so melodramatic and absurd." After viewing the show during a "tough time" in their life, however, they were "in love" with it. Even rewatching the show gives them "that warm feeling and comfort." Tall-Move6136 is sensitive to the hybrid genre of *Jane the Virgin* ("drama, romance, suspense, action, comedy") and to its complex characters ("all . . . have flaws"). Finally, the poster makes a key identification: "i could relate to the Villanueva women considering i'm Hispanic, and it felt like home watching a show that was so relatable."

The final respondent's emphasis is different again. She was also suspicious of the concept: "I remember rolling my eyes at the idea of such a ridiculous show." But Rosalina_10 writes that "it helped me with lots of moments in my life," some of them very precise. "A new mom when [she] started watching," the poster was aided at a difficult time by the episode in which Jane stops pumping breast milk. This enabled the viewer herself to "not feel so much guilt over quitting." Rosalina_10 also mentions the linguistic aspect we have explored in scholarly writing earlier in this chapter:

> [The series] showed a family dynamic where the younger generation spoke English to the Spanish speaking relatives as normal as well. I grew up speaking English even though I fully understand and speak Spanish and was made fun of quite a bit for it. Seeing Jane speak English to her abuela was nice.

While the first poster is sensitive to *Jane the Virgin*'s romance and the second to its hybrid genre and ambivalent characters, the third, beyond fantasy and fiction, makes a deeply felt connection between the show and her everyday experience as a Latina mother, writing quite simply: "I used the advice to help my own life." The televisual text and social context of *Jane the Virgin* come together here in a moving public pedagogy on young female existence.

INTERMISSION 3
THE SECOND SEASON FINALE ("CHAPTER FORTY-FOUR")

Alba, Jane, and Xiomara at the first wedding.

Michael and Jane recite their vows.

Luisa and Rose (Sin Rostro), who reveals her disguise.

If *Jane the Virgin* is, as I suggested earlier, a fond parody of the telenovela, the special wedding episode that serves as a finale to the second season must be especially significant. After all, Latin American serials, among them *Jane the Virgin*'s Venezuelan precursor *Juana la virgen*, almost inevitably end with a white wedding, even when that traditional conclusion is updated. Six years before Jane's eventful nuptials, *Las Aparicio* (Cadenatres/Argos, 2010), also a female-centered show, climaxed with a lesbian ceremony in Mexico City's real-life town hall shortly after marriage equality was approved in the capital.

As a US-style series and not a telenovela, *Jane the Virgin* had not yet reached even its halfway mark on May 16, 2016, when it finally married off Jane and Michael. As a progressive show targeting younger women, it needed to combine the familiar pleasures of the marriage plot with ongoing feminist, Latinx, and queer themes, which are smartly subversive of old-timey romance. Yet, as we shall see, the epic "Chapter Forty-Four" expertly juggles the mixed registers of drama, comedy, and jaw-dropping suspense, while offering dizzying plot twists and a cliff-hanger that even the Narrator could hardly anticipate. Echoing the words of a most unexpected character in the final moments, Latin Lover tells us simply that "it is time to go" (until season three begins, that is).

The episode's first scene starts, as so often, with a flashback, or rather two. We see young Jane listening to and enthralled by the story of her abuela's wedding and then glimpse the pretty period scene ourselves, back in Venezuela. Alba's Spanish-language narration stresses Latina migration and continuity from the home country to the USA. The day after her wedding, which will prove to have been not quite as perfect as the grandmother first suggests, she and her new husband set off for a new country. Then comes a knowing callback to the first season premiere: Jane and Michael kiss passionately on a bed just as they did a year before. As in that first episode, they hold back from having sex, with some difficulty. The difference is that now they only have one day to wait. Or so they think.

Romance gives way to comedy. Rogelio, the father of the bride, is busy organizing the wedding on his phone. An uncooperative Bruno Mars may have played at the Super Bowl, but he should remember that this is "the Super Bowl of weddings." Jokey hashtags flash on-screen, satirizing the nuptials: #hisbigday and #everyboysdream. Another warm moment, when baby Mateo walks for the first time, is set against a further comic episode. Xiomara, who has just unwisely slept with Rogelio's rival telenovela star Esteban, receives a "sex basket" from him. It includes "Este-Buns" for hotdogs that are, according to their packaging, "extra-firm" and "extra-long." Meanwhile, Jane praises with quiet sincerity the "actual sacrament of marriage" that is so plainly profaned by her mother, father, and, we will learn, even her devout grandmother.

Soon the three generations of Villanueva women will be sitting on a bed together, their group shot reminiscent of the first season finale at the hospital. Now Alba tells the true tale of her wedding: how an outraged guest ripped off the bride's veil, revealing that "Alba no es virgen" (that word again). The stern matriarch of the pilot had, unlike Jane, already had sex with another man before the sacred ceremony with her beloved fiancé, and the veil Alba just gave Jane, claiming it was worn by generations of Villanueva women before her, was in fact bought at random at an American flea market, as the original was torn up in Venezuela. Hearing this fond deconstruction of marital bliss, the three women laugh, happy and complicit.

The feminist theme continues in the next sequences. Loyal to her professional ambitions, Jane has decided to meet her university adviser even on her wedding day to propose a new topic for her thesis in creative writing. Rejecting romance, Jane will now write the story of her grandparents' struggles as they trekked from Venezuela to the USA. The pitch is successful, but on helping Jane with the back buttons on her wedding gown, the somewhat stereotypical professor says: "I feel like I'm locking you into the patriarchy." When she congratulates her student, it is on the approval of her thesis proposal, not her marriage.

Inevitably, after this academic encounter Jane will be late for the ceremony, and because of car troubles, she will be forced once more to take the bus. Here there is a callback to the first season (both the premiere and the finale), except that now it is not Rogelio who comes to life in an ad but his nemesis Esteban. Beyond the in-laws, this special episode cannot neglect the series' main structuring device, which the Narrator calls in this season "the mother of love triangles." On the steps of the church, with Jane in her gorgeous white gown and Rafael in a dapper cobalt-blue suit, he declares his love for her and begs her not to marry Michael. Except that, sensitive to her current happiness, he doesn't really. The scene we see is just his fantasy, or the fantasy of at least half of *Jane the Virgin*'s faithful fans, those who are unconditionally #teamrafael even as Jane weds another.

At the beginning of the delayed ceremony, the three generations of women walk down the aisle together, in complementary shades of white, pink, and peach. Jane's father, Rogelio, is seated on a pew, as the rehearsal revealed that there was no space for him to walk alongside his daughter and her indispensable mother and grandmother. Fades to white throughout the sequence—apparently signaling a loss of consciousness—recall once more the birth scene from the first season finale. Jane next speaks her rather brief vows in English, but most surprisingly, Michael pronounces his in grammatically perfect but sexily accented Spanish (he has never spoken Spanish in the series before). As ever, the importance of the Villanuevas' heritage is carefully stressed at this key moment by having an English speaker take Spanish seriously enough to memorize his lines in that language for the vital ceremony.

After this scene of pure, heartfelt romance comes another of comically subversive magical realism. When Jane places her bouquet at a statue of the Virgin Mary, she, the choir, and the congregation sing out to her in liturgical style: "Go have sex, Jane." The reception is equally jolly. Jane and Michael have their first dance to a Bruno Mars ballad played at full length (some fans complain the camera shows the star musician too much and neglects their favorite characters). Then father Rogelio and daughter Jane dance, expertly and humorously, to a more raucous rap track. There is an unusual meta element here, as the reception takes place in the facsimile of the Villanueva home that Rogelio has had built on his soundstage. As the happy couple dances, we can see, beyond the comforting, flowery domesticity, the ominously bare walls and ceiling of the studio building.

Now the last minutes of the episode shift to more troubling plotlines. Xiomara and Rogelio cannot be reconciled, as he still wants the baby she does not. Ironically, she will in this finale episode prove to be pregnant after her one-night stand with Esteban. Petra's twin sister Anežka comments, also ominously, on one of her sister's twin daughters: "She has your sense of humor. Laughing at others' tears." Then in a truly dizzying twist, Anežka takes the place of her sister, whom she has paralyzed and consigned to a hospital with locked-in syndrome. Punning wildly, the on-screen hashtag here reads #petrafied. In rapid succession, Michael, seeking ice for champagne in the hotel hallway on his wedding night, will be shot in the chest by his police partner Susanna, and Susanna reveals that she is really Rose, the mastermind known as Sin Rostro, whom all believe to be dead. Tearing off her somewhat unlikely face mask and wig, Rose solemnly tells her ex-lover Luisa, who impregnated Jane so long ago: "Ours is the greatest love story ever told."

Beyond the cliff-hanger of Michael's shooting, concluding the season with this idiosyncratic lesbian affair (Rose is a multiple murderer and Luisa is a recovering alcoholic) is no doubt the biggest and most knowing betrayal of the wedding plot by *Jane the Virgin*'s writers' room and creator Jennie Snyder Urman. It is striking that the subreddit's discussion of this long-awaited episode on the night of the broadcast focuses as much on the supporting characters as on the main heterosexual and newly married couple ("r/JaneTheVirginCW").

One poster writes: "Petra this season has been one of the strongest characters. It's sad to see her get fooled by the one person [her twin sister] with whom she thought she could finally have a close familial relationship because she never had that with her mother" (compsci17). Others discuss the thesis adviser, a minor figure: "i hate how this show views feminism sometimes" (shewhotalksalot). Or again: "they had to come up with this frustrating stereotype" (name deleted). Yet another focuses on Xiomara's pregnancy and makes an accurate prediction: "The writers might use it as a chance to talk about abortion" (ctadgo). Fans who are #TeamLuisa are glad that Rafael's sister has returned: "Luisa is back but we lost Susanna" (kat6883); or again, "that reveal [of the disguise] was utterly ridiculous" (jesuisunchien). Several posters are skeptical of the Susanna-Rose revelation, the kind of extreme plot twist that Urman associates, wrongly perhaps, with the telenovela.

As to the central couple, there is a positive consensus around the bridegroom's performance, with many posters acknowledging their tears: "Michael's Spanish-language vows were legitimately touching. So sweet" (name deleted); or "this honestly made me tear up" (curly_joe3); or again "my little Latino heart melted in a second" (trotodile). One writes simply: "I cried" (DejaYou87). However, some fans feel betrayed by Michael's subsequent shooting, even as they (mis)quote an early line from the Narrator, which clearly anticipated the tragic event: "He would love her until the day he died. No. Not OK with this" (NonaSweets). Others creatively anticipate the creators' motivations and their implicit pact with the audience: "This episode left me feeling certain that he's not dead. The JtV writers are many things, but they aren't heartless, and Jane being left a sexless widow after such a warm and wonderful wedding just doesn't fit the tone of the show" (breadconference). *Jane the Virgin*'s fans thus proved as agile as the show's creators in juggling different registers and genres. However, as we shall see, those who faithfully shipped Jane and Michael would, like Jane herself, face disappointment once more as the series developed.

3

GENERIC AFFILIATION / FAMILY FILIATION

In this chapter we delve more into the close connection between *Jane the Virgin* and the telenovela genre. This connection is acknowledged in the overarching narrative of Jane's family drama or melodrama but is also integrated into the scenes where characters gather around their TV set to watch Spanish-language faux *novelas* filmed in Miami, mostly starring Jane's father Rogelio. The show's affiliation with the telenovela genre is thus closely linked to the familial connections within its plot, even as it mirrors the career of real-life telenovela star Jaime Camil. In "Chapter Fourteen," Rogelio is offered a lead role in a telenovela back in Mexico but, to stay close to Jane and Xiomara, he remains in the US as a supporting player in his nemesis Esteban's tacky space opera, *Pasión intergaláctica* ("Intergalactic Passion"). In "Chapter Forty-Six," having been rejected for a humiliating three-episode arc on *Hawaii Five-O* because of his accent, he vows in a "crossover moment" to bring his Mexican serials to the US market. This lengthy professional process will be explored right up until the series finale some fifty-four episodes later, when Rogelio becomes an American star with the premiere of his English-language telenovela adaptation, *This Is Mars* (the title is a comically inappropriate reminiscence of lachrymose family drama *This Is Us* [NBC, 2016–22]).

When Rogelio first pitches the American version of *The Passions of Santos* in Hollywood, to The CW no less, Jane asks in a typically nonchalant meta moment of the little-known network that is broadcasting her own show: "What's The CW? Like a streaming thing?" ("Chapter Forty-Seven"). In "Chapter Seventy-Five," guest star Eva Longoria, playing an imperious version of herself, muses to Rogelio: "Taking the most popular show from Latin America and importing it here? I like the sound of that. We can lean into the twists and turns and call it an *homage*" (that last word pronounced with a fancy French accent). Inside and outside *Jane the Virgin*, then, transnational TV traffic is ubiquitous. And, typically nuanced, *Jane the Virgin* acknowledges that US television also has its own overemotional genres. "Chapter Twenty-Four" is staged as a mock episode of *The Bachelorette* (ABC, 2003–present) in which a sequined, tipsy version of Jane tells her everyday opposite number to make up her mind already and give a rose to one of her two rival suitors. Later, in season three, Rogelio will star in an absurdly melodramatic American reality show with his fake wife, Darci.

Discussion as to the nature of the telenovela is typically built into *Jane the Virgin*'s whip-smart script. When Jane, as a new intern, writes her first scene for *The Passions of Santos* in "Chapter Eleven," it is critiqued by clueless Rogelio but praised by savvy Dina (Judy Reyes), the showrunner. Ironically, both cite the same reason: "There's not a lot of yelling and crying." After this disagreement, it is no surprise that Jane raises a barely perceptible eyebrow at Rogelio's statement in the "Telemasivo" studio: "Everyone wants to work in television."

New writer Jane will next be asked to script a bloody finale to *The Passions of Santos* after Rogelio is fired from his own show. However, despite her time writing for TV, she will remain true to her dream of success in the print medium. This tension between TV image and printed text is a source of wry humor throughout the series. For example, in "Chapter Forty-One" a producer suggests using title cards in an episode of Rogelio's time-travel telenovela, which includes faux silent movie sequences. He replies in Spanish: "No one wants to read when they watch television." The sentence is translated into English in subtitles, which we read while watching television.

Here it is worth returning to the original Spanish-language serial, *Juana la virgen*, which is at the time of writing streaming at full length on YouTube but without English subtitles. The telenovela boasts surprising differences with the more familiar remake. The Venezuelan *Juana la virgen* tells the story of Juana Pérez (Daniela Alvarado), a seventeen-year-old girl who, like the older Jane, excels academically and is a devoted daughter. She lives, like Jane once more, with her mother, here called Ana María (Marialejandra Martín), who had her out of wedlock. Ana María is impulsive and reckless (Xiomara is more sympathetic). Juana also lives with her grandmother, Azucena (Aura Rivas), who remains bitter about being abandoned by her husband long ago. Although the grandmother is a breadwinner, she spouts conservative ideas about gender roles ("Soccer playing is for men") that clash with the feminist ideals of Juana ("If it weren't for biology, we women would be exactly the same as men"). Juana's handsome uncle, Manuel (Juan Carlos Alarcón), who has no equivalent in the US series, serves as a male confidant in the female household.

On the other side of the story, we find Mauricio de la Vega (Ricardo Álamo), who shares a surname with Rogelio de la Vega in *Jane the Virgin* (perhaps a sly reference in the remake to the original). Mauricio is a young and handsome entrepreneur who edits a magazine. He is shown shirtless in bed in his very first shot, before exercising in his personal gym and picking at an exquisite breakfast with his wife on their private patio. Mauricio is married to blond vixen Carlota Vivas (Roxana Díaz), a member of the wealthy family that controls the business empire that includes Mauricio's magazine. Carlota's sinister magnate father is called Rogelio (note again a name that will be familiar to viewers of the US remake). True to its credit sequence, which features a sperm and ovum, *Juana la virgen* is pragmatic and explicit about sex. In the premiere episode, Carlota tells her friend complacently that

Mauricio's post-cancer infertility does not affect his performance in bed—quite to the contrary, he knows just how to satisfy a woman.

Juana la virgen consists of an extended 153 daily episodes, each filling a one-hour time slot. The lengthy running time requires a larger cast than the shorter US series to pad out the central drama, with the opening credits featuring the names of twenty adult actors, plus assorted infants and guest stars. Broadcast free to air in Venezuela over seven months, from March 14 to October 16, 2002, *Juana la virgen* featured seasoned writer and creator Perla Farías, who will get a "based on" credit in *Jane the Virgin*, and young star Daniela Alvarado—both of whom had already earned recognition for their work in local serials. Two traditional elements of the initial premise will be shared by the US remake: a romance that transcends class boundaries, here involving the humble Pérez and the wealthy Vivas family into which Juana's inadvertent inseminator has married; and a love triangle featuring the charming Mauricio, his superficial blond wife, and our modest heroine, the feisty brunette Juana Pérez. Note the commonplace surname, unlike the relatively rare "Villanueva." The local press describes the central narrative of the original as romantic, striking a balance between the plausible and the unbelievable, a delicate tonal mixture that the US version also strives to achieve (Hernández 2006). If the Venezuelan Juana seems less engaging than the American Jane, however, it is perhaps because of her relative youth. As a teenager, she is inevitably less developed as a character than her adult opposite number.

Examining the trade press, we gain insights into the industrial context within which *Juana la virgen* emerged. This was a critical period after the authoritarian populist Hugo Chávez rose to power in 1999 and before he removed the irksome broadcaster RCTV from linear TV in Venezuela in 2007 (O'Boyle 2007, 21). In spite of its struggles with the national government, RCTV had exported Venezuela's most popular telenovelas to some eighty countries (Serafini 2007, 1). In the company's outpost in Miami, Jorge Granier, the managing director of RCTV Internacional, would celebrate the extensive library of content at his disposal (Marechal and de la Fuente 2012, 16). This included around three hundred shows that were ripe for remakes. Among the eight formats brought to the US, it was *Juana la virgen* that stood out.

Jane the Virgin remains an exceptional case, as no other RCTV production achieved such success outside its home country. Typically, the remake's dialogue fondly skewers this trend in transnational TV traffic and remakes, a topic that is of course absent in the original serial. When Rogelio reunites with Xiomara in "Chapter Two," he tells her: "I became an international star just a few years ago. Imagine the disservice to the world if I had given up!" Much later, in "Chapter Eighty," he will struggle to keep control over the US adaptation of *The Passions of Santos* when American star River Fields, played by self-mocking guest star Brooke Shields, haughtily objects to "too much crazy stuff" and classic telenovela tropes like amnesia. Fields will later, cannily and dishonestly, take credit for supporting the show and its creator, her underpaid Latinx costar, in *People en Español* magazine ("Chapter Eighty-Four").

The Venezuelan serial is ambivalent about its heroine's decision to abandon her dream due to the unplanned pregnancy, in this case Juana's plans to study photography at a college in Los Angeles (the TelevisaUnivision remake of 2024 sticks closely to the original Juana's predilection for photography and motorbikes, absent in the US version). In contrast, Jane's more modest ambition is to attend graduate school in her hometown of Miami, which she can achieve despite her pregnancy. Yet Juana comes from a more deprived background than Jane. The Venezuelan grandmother helps to support her household by selling empanadas out of the family home, which are delivered to customers by a child worker. In contrast, the Venezuelan American abuela supports her household with steady jobs outside it. Only the most ambitious of students from Juana's social class could have set her sights on winning a scholarship at an American university.

Juana la virgen's premiere episode features graphic animation of the insemination process, no doubt intended to further the sex education or public pedagogy of its younger viewers. Despite such modernizing elements, the original serial does eventually provide the requisite romantic ending. It is no surprise that in the serial's finale, Juana and Mauricio enjoy a classic white wedding. It is a conventional sequence we might contrast with Jane's more dramatic nuptials with Michael and, much later, Rafael. At the start of each daily episode, the lyrics to the theme tune of *Juana la virgen* will remind us of the simple comforts of enduring romance: "I only want to live by your side."

Despite its references to the telenovela genre, *Jane the Virgin* follows the American format as a weekly series blending comedy and drama. As mentioned earlier, there is no Michael equivalent in the original version, just as the remake lacks an opposite number for Juana's hunky uncle, Manuel. Yet there are similarities. Juana's hobby of photography is parallel to Jane's pursuit of a writing career, and Juana will be an intern at the magazine just as Jane will be at the TV studio. Juana will also take photos of the bloody aftermath of a shooting in the first week, initiating an early criminal plotline parallel to the murderous machinations of Sin Rostro, albeit in a much less baroque register.

Three references to telenovelas in the dialogue of "Chapter Two" of *Jane the Virgin* highlight the role the genre plays within the US series from the start. In the first reference, during a discussion of whether the family should meet Petra, abuela compares her to "Catalina Creel," perhaps Mexico's most notorious telenovela villain. Creel, who wears a distinctive eye patch, was featured in Televisa's classic title *Cuna de lobos* ("Cradle of Wolves," Televisa, original 1996; remake 2019) and will be name checked once more as the series approaches its finale ("Chapter Ninety-Eight"). The telenovela serves here as a kind of lingua franca for the Latinx characters throughout *Jane the Virgin*, a repertoire of familiar shortcuts to understanding. A little later in the second episode, Michael promises Jane a "big telenovela gesture" in her locker room: He'll fill it "with flowers or leopards." This takes us back to our first sight of Rogelio's TV studio, where an unlikely leopard is on the loose. Less exotically but more endearingly, Michael's touching gesture will be simply to play romantic music on his phone for him and Jane to kiss to.

The third and final reference is a comic tag at the episode's end. Grandmother Alba bursts into Xiomara's bedroom to find her in bed with Rogelio, whom the abuela knows only from *The Passions of Santos*, which the family watches together. In her surprise, she addresses him by his character's title: "¡El Presidente!" While this humorous exclamation suggests that the older woman cannot distinguish between fiction and reality, Alba soon understands that her daughter is having an affair with the celebrity. Research on women watching telenovelas together has shown that, far from being blinded by romantic fantasy, real-life mothers use their favorite shows to educate their daughters on love and romance (Orozco Gómez 2001, 49). As ever, *Jane the Virgin* slyly incorporates this process into its own plot. Rogelio will solve a quarrel between Xiomara and Jane by restaging their conflict as a telenovela episode in the Telemasivo studios ("Chapter Forty"), and Alba will tell her boyfriend that she loves telenovelas because years ago they made her feel closer to her rebellious teen daughter: "we shared this time together every night" ("Chapter Sixty-Two").

This ambivalent scene, at once moving and everyday, suggests that telenovelas remain as a genre more diverse than *Jane the Virgin* would generally have us believe. On December 29, 2023, Álvaro Cueva, Mexico's most respected TV critic, offered an inventory of that year's telenovelas in his home country (Cueva 2023). Cueva defends the genre from the prejudice whereby *fifís* ("high-class snobs") dismiss broadcast *novelas* as being just for *nacos* ("low-class trash") yet rave over series streamed by Netflix. In 2023, he writes, Mexicans could see educational serials (including the latest edition of the *Vencer* franchise, which I mentioned earlier) but also supernatural *novelas* about demonic sects. One title is "erotic," another "innocent," while a third "radically empowers women." A fourth "reevaluates older adults," as *Jane the Virgin* will do in its later seasons when prim Alba is given a makeover and a romantic interest. Mexican *novelas*, Cueva concludes, have treated politics, Alzheimer's, lesbianism, and religious fanaticism. All this in just one year and one country.

Returning to our remake, the parody telenovelas in *Jane the Virgin* add much to the series' visual and narrative pleasure and to its bilingualism. However, they also testify to the variety of an unfashionable genre that is praised still by Cueva in 2023. First comes *The Passions of Santos*, the show on which Xiomara recognizes the long-lost Rogelio and on which he plays the lavender-uniformed president of the nonsensically named "Ecuadoras del Norte" ("Northern Equators"). He loves his character's costume so much that he is still wearing it when he reveals his paternity to Jane in a bridal store ("Chapter Four"). El Presidente's proposal of marriage to an on-screen fiancée on his show within the show mirrors Jane's proposal to Michael.

A Christ-like Rogelio-as-Santos is seen in an ad on the bus that rushes the pregnant Jane to the hospital in the first season finale, above a tagline that reads "He is Risen." In "Chapter Nine," the cast will gather for the fictional Paloma prize-giving ceremony (real-life equivalents include the International Emmy Award for Best Telenovela in the US and the Premios TVyNovelas in Mexico). Here, as is typical, Rogelio will say the quiet part out loud: "The recognition is nothing. The award is everything." Sadly, he will lose to his gleeful archrival Esteban ("I think of Rogelio as family . . . like a father"). In real life, Camil had also lost when nominated three times for his Mexican telenovelas. However, Rogelio's first faux *novela*, *The Passions of Santos*, was granted the rare honor of a novel version crafted by Urman and her writers' room. It was released in dual English and Spanish versions on online writing community Wattpad, as extra content to reward Rogelio ("Ro") superfans (Jarvey 2015). Later, Rogelio, who has been blown off by his guest Jane, will sadly walk his signature lavender carpet alone at the Miami premiere of his time-travel telenovela, *Tiago a través del tiempo* ("Tiago Through Time," "Chapter Thirty-Five"). The disastrous launch of his final title, *This Is Mars*, makes for a spectacular near finale much later in "Chapter Ninety-Eight."

Over the five seasons of *Jane the Virgin*, Rogelio and his nemesis Esteban will star in fake telenovelas as diverse in theme and genre as those cited in real life by critic Álvaro Cueva. The traditional romance *The Passions of Santos* is matched by the English-language remake *The Passions of Steve and Brenda*, where Rogelio costars in season four with "America's sweetheart" River Fields as unlikely "co-presidents of the United States" in a heart-shaped Oval Office. In his time-travel *novela*, Rogelio materializes in such significant places as New York's Stonewall Inn on the night of the uprising ("Chapter Thirty-Two"). He also costars with Jane's crush Fabian and his rival Esteban in another period show loosely based on *Gulliver's Travels*. Its tagline translates to: "Two little men. One giant love."

In *Pasión intergaláctica*, protagonist Esteban will humiliate second stringer Rogelio by dressing him in his least favorite color. While Rogelio doesn't "pop in peach," Esteban "pops against peach" ("Chapter Fifteen"). Rogelio will next be reduced to a disembodied head bobbing in space ("Chapter Twenty"). In the historical romance *Fernando e Isabel*, Esteban impersonates, with extravagant implausibility, one of Spain's most celebrated monarchs, while Rogelio will be forced quite literally to play the Fool ("Chapter Twenty-Eight" and "Chapter Twenty-Nine"). In the latter episode, an indignant Rogelio will also ride his horse straight out of the TV studio when obliged to appear in a cliched cowboy *novela* titled *El rancho de mi corazón* ("Ranch of My Heart").

While all these references feed into *Jane the Virgin*'s expert comic tone, telenovelas have a deeper importance for the series' diverse fans, as shown by their discussions on the subreddit. A search on January 8, 2024, for the term "telenovela" in the *Jane the Virgin* subreddit reveals a sophisticated response to the genre and a certain measure of didacticism: a desire by Spanish-speaking connoisseurs to share their knowledge with English-speaking fans. When one poster asks: "Have you seen a latino [*sic*] telenovela before watching Jane?" respondents answer that Jane is "tame" compared to real *novelas* and that "my grandma always had telenovelas playing when I was growing up." One British, Canadian, or Australasian fan posts a photo of their TV set with a plate of grilled cheese in the foreground ("Watching my favourite telenovela with my favourite food"). Another user provides a YouTube link to a notorious scene of melodrama in Mexican *novela María, la del barrio* ("Humble Maria," Televisa, 1995), a meme known in shorthand as "Maldita lisiada" ("Damned cripple [*sic*]"). While one user says they watched Televisa titles on trips to Mexico, another reminisces about the popularity of *novelas* in their native Croatia. Lending humorous support to this Slavic connection within the show itself, in "Chapter Seven" Petra, her mother, and their hostage watch *The Passions of Santos* dubbed into their native Czech.

On other subreddit threads, expert fans focus on the differences between rival genres ("telenovela vs. series") or ask for recommendations of telenovelas (connoisseurs give lists). One user asks a question that also puzzled me—"Why does the crew on Rogelio's telenovela speak English?"—while another "spotted our favorite telenovela star in a Spanish textbook" (it is a photo of a young Jaime Camil in Mexico's version of *Ugly Betty*, *La fea más bella* ["The Most Beautiful Ugly Girl," Televisa, 2006–7]). Several other posts refer to the use of telenovelas in Spanish-language learning for English speakers, a further kind of public pedagogy for the US audience. We will recall a flashback sequence in "Chapter Six." Jane and Michael first meet when the police officer is called out to Jane's rowdy twenty-first birthday party. On that magical night he asks her what she likes about telenovelas and, as they watch TV, she interprets the Spanish dialogue for him. Seeing flakes fall on-screen and anticipating her still-distant novel, she adds: "Snow makes everything more romantic."

Finally, the awareness of telenovela as a genre makes fans of the US dramedy conscious of its tropes. One fan cites "evil twins" as a typical plotline. This motif is already featured in *Jane the Virgin*'s first season, when Jane must cope with her precocious, malicious half sisters (Rogelio's daughters from a previous marriage), and when Petra's secret lover, murdered by the deadly ice sculpture of a marlin, appears to have a live identical sibling. In the second season, Petra will encounter her dowdy, klutzy, and finally sinister twin, Anežka, who has sold the family donkey to fund her flight from Prague to Miami. Later, in the same season, Petra herself will give birth to identical blond twins. Jennie Snyder Urman identified this twin trope as the kind of "extreme storyline" she would incorporate into her remake from the original genre.

Another fan ventures into a disturbingly reflexive dimension. In "Did we watch the telenovela?" a poster speculates that the entire series is an adaptation of Jane's novel. They suggest that Jane's son, a now adult Mateo, "has a role in the adaptation of his mother's book." This "makes it seem that we are watching actors playing the characters (which I know we are in real life!)." The supposed cheesy melodrama of telenovelas gives way here to dizzying perspectivism in which the limits of reality and fiction are called into question. This fan's meta suggestion has a similar effect to the moment in "Chapter Thirty-Eight" when the camera pulls back to reveal that Jane's familiar home is a set built on a soundstage. While the original house is being remodeled, Rogelio has (supposedly) had it reconstructed as a venue for Jane and Michael's wedding reception.

Next comes the question of the dubbing of *Jane the Virgin* into Spanish, a round trip for the original Venezuelan concept that was of course translated from Spanish into a mainly English-language remake. In their analysis of linguistic variation in the dubbing of *Jane the Virgin*, Bélgica García Osorio and Alicia Karina Bolaños Medina acknowledge the difficulty of the task faced by the dubbers (Bolaños Medina and García Osorio 2018). This problem of translation is heightened because there are two versions of the dubbed series: one for the Spanish European market and one for Latin America. Interestingly, the version for Spain retains the original voice of Ivonne Coll as the abuela while the version for Latin America substitutes a Latin American actor whose accent is identical to those of the rest of the cast. It also eliminates both Alba's distinctive idioms in Spanish and her vanishingly rare words in English (the iconic "grilled cheese") (Medina and Osorio 2018, 89–90).

What is striking is that these professional scholars, unlike the amateur fans on Reddit, do not distinguish between "series" and "telenovela" and claim wrongly that characters in the original series speak "Spanglish." They use a dismissive term employed only in Spain for telenovelas—"culebrón" or "big snake"—and state chauvinistically that Jane "has no accent" in the European version, as she was dubbed into "standard Peninsular Spanish" (Medina and Osorio 2018, 96). They also claim that the "overacted . . . Latin American accent" given to Xiomara in the version intended for Spain is inherently comic. These Spanish scholars, then, are insensitive to the dramatic and emotional elements of *Jane the Virgin* that affect American fans so deeply, seeing the show only as a crude comedy or melodrama. They thus rely on the broad, negative stereotypes of telenovelas and, indeed, of Latin Americans, that *Jane the Virgin* works so hard to subvert. The unique bilingual achievement of the original series seems impossible to reproduce in a dubbed version, even for Spanish-speaking audiences who share a measure of cultural heritage with US Latinxs.

INTERMISSION 4
THE FIFTH SEASON PREMIERE ("CHAPTER EIGHTY-TWO")

Michael as Jason and Jane on his return.

Jane's shock at Michael's return.

Rafael's concern for Jane.

Jane after her monologue.

Faithful fans had to wait almost a year for the fifth and final season of *Jane the Virgin* to premiere on March 27, 2019, and they needed to wrestle during that extended period with perhaps the most disturbing of cliff-hangers in the whole series: the return of Jane's dead husband Michael at the end of the fourth season finale. It is not clear if the characters or the audience are more shocked by the reappearance of a figure whom they have collectively mourned throughout season four. Some #TeamMichael enthusiasts even say on Reddit that they have barely paid attention to their former "comfort show" since his death. In the absence of fan favorite Michael, Jane has recovered from her trauma (aided by a three-year jump in story time), dated unsuitable suitors (actor Fabian and comic book artist Adam), and finally reconciled with a thoughtful and responsible Rafael whose arc has taken him far indeed from his opening playboy machismo. In this episode, Jane is anticipating, once more, a proposal of marriage.

The first sequences of the momentous "Chapter Eighty-Two," directed by star Gina Rodriguez (an executive producer of the show at this time) and written solely by series creator Jennie Snyder Urman, are properly somber in tone. Beginning as so often with flashbacks, we see Jane and her family on successive visits to the cemetery on the Day of the Dead, cleaning the tombs of first her grandfather Mateo and then her husband Michael. Movingly, the child Mateo, named for his grandfather, is present for the last visit. Although the dialogue takes care to note that this is not one of the family's own Venezuelan traditions, we glimpse Mexican mourners in full skull face paint. This disturbing image will recur later in the episode, projected in turn onto the visages of Michael (now called Jason) and Jane herself in an example of the series' recurrent trope of magical realism. The theme of amnesia in this episode has also been trailed in the previous season as a telenovela trope essential to Rogelio's American remake of *The Passions of Santos*.

In the first present-day sequence, we return to Rafael's gloomy apartment, where Jane confronts Jason, actor Brett Dier now transformed into a morose, taciturn dog lover from Montana. Jason's ominous canine replaces Michael's beloved cat, who will play a prominent role in Jane's forthcoming monologue. An explanatory cutaway to sexy, sinister Rose (otherwise known as Sin Rostro) speaking to Rafael from prison establishes that the series' perennial master criminal faked Michael's death and turned him into amnesiac Jason through electroshock treatments. A second, minor cliff-hanger from the last episode is now resolved in a more comic key. We learn that the person whom Petra's lover JR shot (out of shot) is only wounded and that it is Petra's ex-husband Milos, an unsympathetic, comic villain. Petra, once herself a toxic villainess, will be given a more heartfelt scene a little later on. Now Jason (previously Michael) visits the family in their once-familiar home. Comedy briefly kicks in again when he fails to recognize Rogelio, who, egomaniacal as ever, was convinced that he alone could cure the amnesiac. A more sober scene at the neurologist's office confirms that the science remains unclear on Jason's condition and the possibility of a cure.

Next comes the celebrated seven-minute single-take of Jane's monologue, which takes up a complete act between two of broadcast TV's traditional commercial breaks. Curiously, it takes place in the cozy kitchen with a silent mother and grandmother looking (hearing) on. Jane, or rather Gina Rodriguez, actor and director, cycles through a bewildering range of emotions here. First comes doubt: is she still really the wife of a husband so long mourned? Next comes grief: To the tearful Jane, the otherwise unrecognizable Jason "smells exactly like Michael." Then anger: Jane yells in distress at her silent family. And, finally, humor: Should she join an "amnesia support group"? The scene seems like a bid for the Emmy acting award that Rodriguez would so unjustly never receive.

Accompanying this virtuoso speech is a full repertoire of physical gestures, sometimes surprisingly humorous. Jane picks up the cat (Michael's cat, unrecognized by Jason) and eats one of her grandmother's arepas (no time to make grilled cheese). She puts the kettle on the stove to make tea only to discover several minutes later that she has failed to turn on the heat. Still talking, she walks right out of frame (out of the kitchen) and returns minus her jeans, wearing only her underpants. This single shot, unparalleled in the whole series, is accompanied by necessarily fluid and complex camera movements that track the actor (are tracked by the director) as she moves repeatedly right and left in the kitchen, and even to the front door to meet the movers. They have come, vainly and ironically, to take Jane's furniture to the new home that she cannot yet share with Rafael, as the reappearance of her old romance has disrupted her new love. Defiantly, movingly, unconvincingly, Jane declares at the end of this sequence shot: "I'm doing great."

The rest of the starring and recurring cast get their dramatic moments too. In the kind of carefully crafted parallelism for which the series' scripts are known, Rafael first consoles a weeping Rogelio, who has lost his "best friend" Michael, and is then consoled himself by Xiomara, still recovering from cancer, as he weeps bitterly for what he takes to be his lost relationship with Jane. Extended flashback sequences, integrated into the present-day plot, deepen the emotional payoff for characters and viewers alike. Jane takes Jason on a "Michael tour" that revisits the highly charged locations of their courtship, including the funfair where they kissed on the Ferris wheel so long ago. Later, Jane, committed to writing even in extremis, recreates more momentous moments as she taps them out on her computer keyboard for us to see: the wedding, the shooting, the funeral. In this last scene, which we have not seen before, Rafael steps up to read the eulogy to Michael that a distraught Jane cannot. Knowing that Michael is still alive (in a manner of speaking) does not prevent her or us from weeping bitterly over lost love.

Yet even in this tragic premiere episode, there are touches of humor that are grotesque and farcical. The wounded Milos has escaped discovery by hiding in Petra's apartment at the Marbella inside a giant teddy bear. When Petra confronts her beloved JR, she is still holding that blood-stained furry costume. Rafael's ex-wife, who here explicitly comes out as bisexual, is given a moving monologue to the lesbian lover she has betrayed and caused to be disbarred. Confessing to a lifetime of lies and deceit, still Petra declares fervently: "I love you." JR refuses to be won over.

This voicing of lesbian love echoes a scene of heterosexual declaration that just precedes it and harks back as far as the now-distant series premiere. Then, a young Jane went in a yellow dress to Michael's workplace to propose marriage to him. Now, a more mature Jane, wearing an equally vivid yellow dress, goes to Rafael's new workplace (having lost control of the hotel, he has just taken a job as a real estate agent to support his family). Once more Jane makes a moving declaration of love, embarrassingly in front of her suitor's colleagues, and in a romantically charged graphic match, a single petal will fall once more from a white flower. Yet this nostalgic episode ends with an unpredictable cliff-hanger. The imprisoned Rose is shown addressing via video screen a group of louche, criminal "angels," all female but one, whom Rose is grooming for further plots. These will no doubt prove as diabolical and as unlikely as her faking Michael's murder.

It is not surprising that this episode was deeply felt by fans. On Reddit there are, exceptionally, over one thousand posts, many citing traumatic or momentous moments in viewers' lives, such as marriages, deaths, and cancer diagnoses ("r/JaneTheVirginCW"). "Chapter Eighty-Two" also attracted special critical attention from the general and specialist press, often focusing on the fact that this was only the second of three times that Gina Rodriguez would serve as director of an episode. *IndieWire* wrote: "That 7-Minute Epic Monologue Is Everything That's Great About the Series," commenting that "the show explores how Jane . . . has grown and the way that one forms a sense of self" (Nguyen 2019). The journalist goes on: "It's an existential dilemma that Jane as a writer can't help but try to categorize." Beyond these big themes, the journalist also calls attention to the "small hilarious details that give the show its emotional authenticity, embracing sentiment without devolving into melodrama" (such as "just walking around without her pants").

This "mastery of tone" comes of course from mastery of technique, as we see in interviews, given with their professional peers, by writer-creator Jennie Snyder Urman and actor-director Gina Rodriguez. Speaking of the "seven-and-a-half-page monologue that Urman wrote and Rodriguez performed and directed in a oner [*sic*]," the showrunner says to *Variety* that before writing she puts herself "in the character's shoes" and explores "the range of human emotion that you would have in that instant" (Turchiano 2019). Content determines form here. Because the revelation was "so huge," it deserved to be shown "in a new, fresh way" different than anything else on the show, that is the single take.

At an earlier date, Rodriguez herself had recounted to *The Hollywood Reporter* her complex process as first-time director of a previous episode (Turchiano 2018). She says: "I found myself enjoying directing and acting [simultaneously] because as a director you're given direct access to . . . what Jennie's looking for and the tone." Yet although she "collaborated with her creator," she also "put her own stamp on the episode." Rodriguez discovered "a system for directing." First, she did one take, watched it on playback, and "fixed everything technically with the camera and with acting or staging or blocking." Then she would take three more takes to "do different levels." Being both in front of and behind the camera at the same time meant she had to do "extra preparation." As a "pretty studious human being" (so like Jane!), she knew "every line of the script" before she set foot on set.

Elsewhere, the fledgling director offers a more personal explanation for her minute preparation: "For Rodriguez, who is of Puerto Rican descent, the decision to direct is important in another sense: representation. Latinos [*sic*] directed just 4% of episodic TV shows in the 2016–17 season" (Villarreal 2018). The theme of this very special episode, namely the way that one forms a sense of self by telling stories, is thus linked to the way in which it was made, to its new, fresh way of exploring emotion and developing a rare creative career for its accomplished star.

4
STARS AND PERFORMANCE

When I took the (totally unofficial) *Jane the Virgin* character test quiz, I was surprised to find out that I was a "Petra":

> You are the epitome of bad girls do it well. You will stop at nothing to get what you want: money, power, and respect. You prefer Prada over retail, and you turn heads wherever you go. ("Which 'Jane the Virgin' Character Are You? Quiz," 2020)

The playful questionnaire, hosted by the aptly named website needsomefun.net, suggests that *Jane the Virgin*'s characters are unchanging archetypes (the epitome of bad, or good, girls and boys). Yet the series itself showcases the characters' continuing development via the performances of their skilled actors. For example, in "Chapter Eighty-Seven," Jane and Petra, once bitter enemies, finally become (as my Reddit correspondent suggested) something like sisters, dancing together onstage at a lesbian nightclub, first clumsily, then joyfully and sexily. In the behind-the-scenes documentary that makes up "Chapter Ninety-Nine," Yael Grobglas talks of "the journey for actors" and the difficulty in saying goodbye to a character like Petra, who, after five long years, came to feel like "a friend." Of course, of the regular cast, Grobglas alone had the actorly burden, or opportunity, of switching between Petra and her twin Anežka, with their very different looks, gestures, and accents, not to mention their dizzying propensity to impersonate one another.

Among so many other things, then, *Jane the Virgin* is also a commentary on acting. Jaime Camil's Rogelio is the focus for the show's continuing satirical commentary on celebrity culture, as a Latin American star with an outsize image of himself who also struggles to succeed in an inhospitable US. In "Chapter Ninety-Six," he attempts to encourage Jane in her still disappointed vocation as a writer by recounting his own apprenticeship in his craft. This takes the form of a protracted shaggy dog story that tells how, long ago, Rogelio "method auditioned" as a homeless man in Mexico City for esteemed director Alejandro González Iñárritu (the role Rogelio describes is clearly reminiscent of indigent hitman El Chivo in *Amores perros* [2000]). After ever more vain and desperate efforts to impress Iñárritu, Rogelio succeeds only in having the director take out a restraining order against him, but the embarrassing scandal that ensues still helps him advance in his career. Performance and self-publicity are thus intimately connected. Yet in the making-of documentary in "Chapter Ninety-Nine," Yvonne Coll (abuela Alba) is keen to make clear that the stylized acting of the telenovela, so often defended by Camil and his "method auditioning" character, is very different from that of a US series like their own.

In this final chapter, then, we explore the performance and extratextual personas of the cast in *Jane the Virgin* through the lens of star studies. According to Richard Dyer, a pioneer in the field, Hollywood stars can be read alternately as social phenomena, as images, and as signs (this last category includes for Dyer the study of both character and performance). Key here are the linked questions of "contradictions" and "multiplicity" (Dyer 1998 [1979], 26, 94). My own primary focus is on Gina Rodriguez, an actor and activist who proudly identifies as "brown" and a Puerto Rican American with close Jewish connections (Goldberg 2014). Her self-presentation in interviews and on social media showcases the contradictory or multivalent appeal she makes to a Latinx identity and community, itself characterized by its hybrid nature. Anticipating the #MeToo movement, Rodriguez used the trade press as a platform to advocate for changing the prevailing beauty standards for women in Hollywood and to promote the interests of Latinas in the entertainment industry. She even took on the role of entrepreneur, cofounding a lingerie startup for women with bodies like herself (Chan 2015).

Gina Rodriguez thus carefully orchestrates the multiple resources marshaled by a star such as entrepreneurship, advocacy, physicality, fashion, social media, performance style, and voice acting (I will return to her distinctive vocal delivery later). Two early interviews with the nascent star in *The Hollywood Reporter* show her already crafting a career as an actor and public figure within the entertainment industry. As the trade journal's "next big thing," even before the premiere of her signature show, Rodriguez announced an impressive, if jocular, ambition: "*Jane the Virgin* Star Gina Rodriguez Wants to Be the Latino Meryl Streep" (Goldberg 2014). Introduced in the article as a graduate of New York University's prestigious Tisch School of the Arts, Rodriguez stresses from the start her social commitment: She "won't play characters unless they serve as role models for young Latinos." She also cites her debt to pioneering performers like Rita Moreno, who was later a guest star on *Jane the Virgin*. Rodriguez embraces a "dual identity," celebrating her origins while refusing to be limited by them: "I am not defined by the fact that my parents speak Spanish or that my skin color is brown." She also reveals her private struggle with thyroid disease from age nineteen: "It was very hard to deal with my weight." An accompanying short video shows the charming Rodriguez being made up for her photo shoot, a glimpse behind-the-scenes for the industry audience that she will later grant to fans on Instagram.

One year later, at the same journal's comedy actress roundtable, Rodriguez is celebrated as a breakout TV star, and she shares the limelight with "the year's hottest television actresses." These include established Anglo contemporaries like Lina Dunham (*Girls*), Amy Schumer (*Inside Amy Schumer*), and Kate McKinnon (*Saturday Night Live*) (Howard 2015).

The women discuss what the magazine calls "weighty topics such as racism and sexism in Hollywood." Once more, Rodriguez cites the professional challenges of her ethnicity: "I'm a brown girl. I have to cross all the lines just to be known." However, she also "poked fun at the notion that she could possibly speak for or generalize the Latino audience," joking: "Actually, I've met every single one of them and they're all related to me" (Howard 2015). Asked if her audience is "too conservative to handle the themes of virginity, Catholicism, abortion, and sex on *Jane the Virgin*," she insists on the viewers' contradictions and multiplicity: "The Latino audience is all over the place. [It] encompasses like fifty different countries. That's why it's kind of hard to talk about them."

At the same time as she sat for these interviews, Rodriguez (or perhaps her staff) was curating a multivalent public image on Instagram, then the most attractive picture-based platform for celebrities. #HereIsGina has at the time of writing 4.4 million followers, testimony to Rodriguez's continuing connection with her admirers. Her account describes the star as an "artist." For fond fans of Jane, the main value of the feed is surely its tantalizing promise of personal intimacy with their beloved star Gina. A key question here is once more women's health and body shape. Rodriguez is seen on the cover of, precisely, *Women's Health*, giving "her guide to major confidence" on April 13, 2016, and on the cover of *Shape* magazine (with two hundred thousand likes) on September 8, 2017. We can take pleasure in following the maturing star from a digital distance until, years after her character, she reveals a real-life baby of her very own (June 18, 2023).

Equally tantalizing, but very different in character, is the access to TV production processes through the lens of a still new star. For example, on March 13, 2014, we glimpse a wall with headshots of the now familiar actors. They are, however, identified by their characters' unfamiliar original names in the show (e.g., Rogelio was "Rubio" and Petra was "Monica"). On her feed, Rodriguez starts to pose with established celebrities, including Latinx luminaries, burnishing her new luster with their more mature reflected glory. She shows herself with established Mexican actor and latterly director Diego Luna as early as March 1, 2014, and with "sister friends" Salma Hayek and Zoe Saldaña on August 13, 2018 (of course, many of the celebrities in her feed also appear as guest stars in the show itself). Rodriguez also engages in assertive but unpreachy progressive politics that chime with the values and issues of her series and no doubt those of her fans. On January 21, 2017, she posted an image at the women's march (her T-shirt's slogan was "Torch Your Bra"), and just one week later, on January 29, 2017, a photo of herself holding a placard reading "Without immigrants there would be no USA."

Still, Rodriguez takes care to appeal to the apolitical pleasure of fashion, the latter a *Jane the Virgin* fan priority that boasts its own subreddit. For example, she is naturally glowing on the cover of *Glamour*'s special "Belleza Latina" issue as "TV's Refreshing New Star" (June 9, 2015) and appears old-school glamorous in a midnight-blue, full-length ball gown at the Golden Globes on January 10, 2016 ("absolute magic"). Social media remains, however, a treacherous game. Rodriguez, the Latina activist and proud "brown girl," was tripped up by a controversy over race when she posted a video in which she used the N-word when heedlessly singing along to an old Fugees track. The polemic made it as far as Mexico, where *El Universal* felt the need to explain to local readers why this was "a serious offense in the United States" ("Gina Rodríguez se disculpa por utilizar palabra racista en video" 2019). Rodriguez apologized profusely, writing on Instagram: "The words that I spoke should not have been spoken . . . I am so deeply sorry for the pain I have caused." The fact that her post received almost two hundred eighty thousand likes suggests that the star skillfully navigated the potential damage to her reputation and was pardoned by her devoted fans.

The versatility of Gina's persona as seen on social media is more than matched in later seasons of *Jane the Virgin* by the volatility of her character Jane, who exhibits extreme contradictions. After the initial youthful exuberance (Jane as a mermaid-waitress flops into the

Marbella pool!), there is a shift in tone toward mourning and melancholia. Jane's new, mature development is in part a response to her mother Xiomara's grueling odyssey through cancer treatment. Responsible as ever in its dedication to public pedagogy, *Jane the Virgin* introduces its audience to a disturbing vocabulary here such as the "cold caps" that seek to prevent the patient's hair loss, at the cost of extreme discomfort, and the "chemo brain" that can shut down a once vivacious personality. The Spanish scholars who tagged "Xo" as a purely comic character would be surprised and shocked by Andrea Navedo's unselfish performance here over so many emotionally draining episodes.

At the same time, there is continuing conflict with Rafael over the coparenting of Mateo. This climaxes when their child is diagnosed as suffering slow development and behavioral issues (an unwelcome surprise to Jane, who was always an excellent student). Michael's sudden death in "Chapter Fifty-Four" will lead to scenes of Jane mourning over an extended period, even though a three-year gap in story time spares viewers the most traumatic period (the time change is signaled to viewers in part by hair design: After Michael's death, Jane adopts a shorter, more mature shag style). Soon Jane will return to dating with the unsuitable Fabian, who belies his unlikely surname ("Regalo del Cielo" means "Heaven's gift"). As a brief but loving wife and grieving widow, she struggles with the unfamiliar experience of no-strings sex with a very dumb hunk who she has nothing in common with (as they watch Netflix together in "Chapter Sixty-One," he asks her: "Did you know Queen Elizabeth was a real person?"). Each of these new developments requires the versatile Rodriguez to modify her performance style and modulate her emotional tone between and within episodes.

With the renewed focus on Jane's son in "Chapter Ninety-One," Mateo is finally diagnosed with attention deficit hyperactivity disorder (ADHD). A conflictive discussion on the appropriate therapy ensues between his parents over several episodes. Should they opt for medication or behavioral treatment? Professional disappointments also pile up in this last season as Jane's second novel is rejected by agents and she discovers, to her horror, that Rogelio had paid to publish her first. Her self-image as a published writer is thus revealed as a fantasy. In "Chapter Ninety-Eight," a tense Jane is trained in a therapeutic technique to reduce stress. This time it is the acupuncture-like EFT, which, we are told, stands for the "emotional freedom technique." It is carried out by rhythmically "tapping" parts of the face and body in sequence. Jane will use it to secretly communicate with Rafael when she is kidnapped by Rose in the latter's last and most spectacular criminal enterprise.

Character arcs thus interact with plot developments in unpredictable ways. In a typically meta moment of the final season, the show makes explicit the five key structural elements of TV scriptwriting, which are highlighted in on-screen titles: the drive, the obstacle, the complication, the resolution, and the cliff-hanger ("Chapter Ninety"). The new close attention to the contradictory psychological interests of the protagonist (her drives, obstacles, and complications) is reinforced by the continuing flashbacks to Jane's girlhood, which began as far back as the pilot and continue as late as the series finale. These recollections seek to establish a psychic motivation for Jane's actions and problems, one that is played with dramatic seriousness by the same Gina Rodriguez who years before had participated in *The Hollywood Reporter*'s comedy actress roundtable.

The theme of mental health thus becomes central to the show's final seasons, for the mother and for the son. It is no accident that the recent book *Latinx TV in the Twenty-First Century* should include an essay focusing on that theme in *Jane the Virgin* and citing Rogelio's healing mantra in its title: Danielle Alexis Orozco's "Inhala, Exhala: Latinas, Mental Health Journeys, and Accessible Shaping Devices" (2022). Orozco praises Jane as a "complex, multidimensional character" (Orozco 2022, 114) and celebrates the way *Jane the Virgin* seeks to "represent the complex discussions of mental health and disability status in Latinx communities" (Orozco 2022, 118). She also highlights the role of the off-screen

Narrator in "disseminat[ing] information about possible therapeutic strategies" for conditions covered in seasons three through five. These include "anxiety, panic attacks, trauma, PTSD [post-traumatic stress disorder], and ADHD" (the author of the article also has this last condition and identifies deeply with the show) (Orozco 2022, 119).

Key here for Orozco is "Chapter Fifty-Six" (described as "One Month After Michael's Death"), in which a distraught Jane receives successful treatment from a therapist. This episode presents the character and audience with another helpful acronym that identifies triggers or stressors for negative emotions that are carefully spelled out for viewers on screen: "HALT" stands for "hungry, angry, lonely, tired" (Orozco 2022, 121). As the Narrator, soon to be identified as the grown version of child Mateo, also confesses to undergoing therapy at this point ("mine was much more awkward"), Orozco perceives a "lineage . . . a new tradition if you will" between mother and son (Orozco 2022, 122). Of course, the effectiveness of this psychic pedagogy relies on viewers' identification with and affection for Jane and Latin Lover, realized by the skilled and affecting performances of a very visible Gina Rodriguez and a discreetly off-screen Anthony Mendez.

Rodriguez effortlessly combines this heartfelt psychological drama with assured screwball humor. In repeated fantasy sequences in later seasons, Jane changes into comic avatars that require the actress to be physically transformed. Special episodes of this type are devoted to a nineteenth-century melodrama based on Jane's first novel, *Snow Falling*; a silent 1920s movie casting Jane as a sloe-eyed vamp; a tacky reality show; and an even tackier electoral debate (Jane and Petra as rival political candidates boasting bouffant hair). In the very late "Chapter Ninety-Three," musical fans are rewarded with a full-scale song and dance number from the whole cast (chorus: "It's love, love, love") starring Jane and featuring choreographed trees. This sequence is a fantasy offshoot of Mateo's calamitous ecologically themed school play.

Rodriguez's wide-ranging versatility throughout *Jane the Virgin* is confirmed by her subsequent roles in cinema and television, which embrace wildly different genres. Yet she retains a distinctive look and, just as important perhaps, a distinctive sound. Gina as Jane has an instantly recognizable voice with an intimate, raspy tone reminiscent of what is called vocal or glottal fry (Parachuk 2024). A professional voice acting website sets out the dangers and pleasures of this technique. Despised by some listeners as a "linguistic fad" like "Valley Girl" or "uptalk," it can damage actors' voices and "distract from their message." Conversely, vocal fry facilitates "relatable communication" and can be "a very powerful tool," sounding "more natural and accessible to the audience" than "a polished, professional HR voice." Moreover, criticism of vocal fry is "disproportionately aimed at younger women." Although these voice professionals make no reference to *Jane the Virgin*, their comments uncannily capture Rodriguez's vocal performance in the creation of a unique character. After all, Jane is a much-criticized young woman who remains, nonetheless, natural, accessible, relatable, and, finally, powerful. And she achieves her professional and personal goals without betraying herself and adopting a polished, human-resources-style voice and persona.

The actors who portray Jane's two competing love interests in the show also hold special interest in this context of performance. Beyond their role as heartthrobs (for Jane and the audience), both reliable Michael and erratic Rafael, as played by Brett Dier and Justin Baldoni, offer insights into the evolving concepts of masculinity and the transition from heedless or clueless youth to responsible maturity. The latter has been outspoken in his efforts to redefine masculinity. The actor's off-screen comments chime with his character Rafael's slow evolution into a more sensitive father, romantic partner, and finally husband in later seasons. Baldoni himself authored a book titled *Boys Will Be Human: A Get-Real Gut-Check Guide to Becoming the Strongest, Bravest, Kindest Person You Can Be* that encourages young men to confront their emotions and fears (Baldoni 2022). One of my fan correspondents on Reddit wrote of Baldoni's kindness when she reached out to him at a difficult time in her life. The final version of Rafael would no doubt have approved of the noble sentiments in Baldoni's book, and its subtitle echoes his character's repeated and supportive advice to Jane: "Be brave."

Other series regulars are also given unexpected arcs, which must be plausibly performed by their actors and accepted by longtime viewers. We have already seen Petra's transition from heterosexual ice queen to passionate lesbian lover, and Jane's pious abuela is also transformed, albeit with glacial slowness, over several seasons. Puerto Rican Ivonne Coll, who plays Alba and is an actress long known for supporting roles in telenovelas, has a lengthy professional biography (an actor's "journey") that feeds into her expert performance on *Jane the Virgin*. An extended interview for the AV Club celebrates how the former Miss Puerto Rico and bit player on film and television "brought immense depth and complexity to a character that challenges how older Latinas are portrayed on screen" (Sava 2018).

Like Rodriguez, Coll is lavish in her praise for showrunner Jennie Snyder Urman, including Urman's risky choice that Alba should speak only in Spanish in the first episodes. Coll was amazed by this decision, as she knew American audiences were reluctant to read subtitles. Ironically, she herself had "spent so much money on [English] diction classes" (Coll, we are told, had also trained with "some of New York City's greatest acting teachers"). Moreover, Alba's experience was alien to Coll's. Coll, as a lifelong US citizen, "had no idea what it [was] to be an immigrant without papers." Conscious of her craft, Coll describes her acting technique in the TV series that gave her such an unexpected big break in her late career. It is a direct communication of emotion: "I think in terms of how I can move the people watching, the same way I would if they were there in person in a theater play. That's my challenge as an actor." This is the kind of skilled emotional intelligence displayed by all the series' regular and recurring performers, even as they negotiate the contradictions of celebrity that are newly perilous in the age of social media.

INTERMISSION 5
THE FIFTH SEASON AND SERIES FINALE ("CHAPTER ONE HUNDRED")

Xiomara, Jane, and Alba on the porch swing.

Petra, Jane, and Rafael at the rehearsal dinner for the second wedding.

Jane's paternal grandmother, Mateo, and Rogelio before the wedding.

Jane and Rafael, the finally happy couple.

"Friends, where to start?" The Narrator's first words in the last episode herald a quick-cut montage, different in style to the familiar recap, signaling that this is a special moment. He accompanies the images by mentioning "the accidental insemination, the love story, the heartbreak, the friendship, the marriages, the family, the career high" (Jane just sold her second novel for half a million dollars), and, finally, the three women. "Yes," he concludes, "at the end of the day, with those three women . . . that's where our story began." We now see Jane, Xiomara, and Alba laughing in the living room. This season and series finale, which poses as a beginning, was broadcast on July 31, 2019, and written solely by executive producer Jennie Snyder Urman.

The flashback proper that follows, a device familiar from so many previous episodes, shows the young Jane watching TV, distraught to discover that, when their final secret is revealed, even telenovelas must come to an end. Why, she asks her mother and grandmother, can't her beloved shows be like the American soaps that go on forever that her friend Lina watches with her family? I recall that on the subreddit one of the respondents to my post on the writing of this book also wrote affectionately of "awesome soaps," not telenovelas, as an essential predecessor of *Jane the Virgin*: "it's love and death and cancer and birth" (Ordinary_Rough_1426).

Xiomara and Rogelio are planning to move to New York City, following the relocation of the production of his much-troubled first network drama in the US. Though Xo has doubts about leaving the family she has never been apart from, Alba tells her to be brave. After all, the abuela left Venezuela for a new life in the US, a much greater challenge than that facing her daughter. Meanwhile, Jane's book manuscript is finally finished and has a new ending (there will be several rewrites). But the last secret of the series proves, unlike those typical of telenovelas, to be a dispiriting one. Rafael's birth parents have been identified, but they are dead: ordinary people who died in the ordinary tragedy of a car accident. This is in marked contrast to the spectacular demise of Rose (Sin Rostro) in the previous episode. After holding Jane hostage in a failed attempt to win back Luisa ("Ours is the greatest love story ever told"), *Jane the Virgin*'s perennial criminal mastermind met a fiery death impaled on an extraterrestrial creature at the premiere of Rogelio's new sci-fi series.

Now we return to the wedding preparations. A happy sleepover with the three children of the now blended family (Jane's son with Rafael, Rafael's twin daughters with Petra) leads into the rehearsal dinner at which Rogelio's formidable mother, played by Rita Moreno, makes a brief and welcome return. Ex-villainess Petra, now Jane's beloved "sister," attempts a jokey speech before uncharacteristically dissolving into tears. Remembering her old self, she admits: "I don't usually wish happiness on other people." Continuing her own dialogue with Latin American serials, Jane tells Rafael that their story together is not a telenovela, as "our wedding is not the ending but the beginning of our lives." Sadly, fans will not see how those lives turn out after this finale.

Now the three generations of women are shown cozily lying on the bed together, as they have been at key points in the past. A flashback montage has the threesome in the familiar living room as Alba contemplates with sadness but resignation the breaking up of her female family (still, she has a new and sexually satisfying husband to share the home with). Soon all three will be crying and holding hands once more on the porch swing. Beyond this deeply felt domestic sentiment, the urgent demands of professional life continue, as ever. Sensible Rafael suddenly acts like Jane has in the past, making a wild trip to her publisher with a new ending to Jane's manuscript on the morning of his wedding. He ends up crashing his car and being arrested by the police.

Echoing the comic tours de force of her wedding to Michael and the birth of Mateo, Jane is now obliged to once again take a city bus to the wedding venue. An image of Rogelio is seen on the side of this bus too, in an ad for his new series with River Fields. Coming to life as before, Rogelio's image now tells Jane to "hop on." Meanwhile, Xiomara calls for the real Rogelio to cross over the street that is clogged with marathon runners to get to the bus. The phrase evokes his recent hard-won success as a crossover TV star in the US, the fulfillment of a long-held professional ambition. The once silly, self-obsessed actor has by now traced a satisfying arc to public and private maturity.

As the guests wait in the pretty exterior location beside the ocean (the other weddings in the series took place inside a church), Petra reconciles with her ex-lover JR with a very public kiss in front of the guests. One last time, lesbian love joins hands here with straight romance on equal terms. Matching the joyful tone, the principal women are dressed here in pretty, pastel gowns: baby blue for Alma and blush pink for Xiomara and Lina, Jane's best friend. The Narrator repeats off-screen that "it should be noted" that Jane's passions are (as back in "Chapter One") family, faith, and grilled cheese sandwiches—but now there is a special addition to the list of passions (Jane is famous for her lists): Rafael, her soon-to-be-husband and the involuntary biological father of her son.

When the happy couple arrives at the venue late after an eventful bus ride, the child Mateo recites a short poem to the guests. He has been coached in this by his great-grandmother, who tells him to project. After his successful performance, she advises him to work as a voice-over artist. Breaking into the first person, Latin Lover tells us: "That's what I did." The riddle of the Narrator's identity is thus finally solved to the satisfaction of fans who had long predicted this outcome. The revelation makes little sense chronologically, as the child Mateo can hardly exist at the same time as the adult Mateo who is narrating his story in a shared present moment. Yet, still, there is poetic justice in having Jane's beloved, accidentally inseminated child, the origin of all the series' action, serve as the Narrator to his mother's emotional roller coaster of a story.

Now the show takes care to pay, as so often, explicit allegiance to its Latin cultural roots. Rogelio offers the couple what he calls a "lazo de novia" (more commonly known as "lazo de boda"), saying it is a Mexican custom. This is an ornamental lasso that will be placed around the couple at one point in the ceremony, symbolically linking them together. Stern and fond abuela Alba, who is officiating this non-Catholic ceremony, speaks, as always, in Spanish. She instructs those guests whom she humorously calls "Spanish-impaired" to read the translation of her words in their programs. Then white petals fall from a tree one last time, the familiar Florida version of snowflakes for Jane the character and Jane the author. Happy wedding photos now show the guests increasingly numerous in each shot, as the large supporting cast gets their final, brief place in the limelight. Even Esteban, Rogelio's once ridiculous rival, proposes to his partner Darci, who is also the mother of Rogelio's baby, thus tying up a final loose end.

Now comes the last shot of the last episode (sorry, "chapter"). Jane and Rafael, still in their wedding finery, are sitting casually on the ground beneath the white-blossomed tree. He asks her: "What happens at the end of your novel?" She replies: "They made it into a telenovela." To which he responds lovingly, playfully: "Well, who would want to watch that?" Jane turns to the camera and winks at the audience, breaking the fourth wall for the first time in a hundred episodes. Ironic yet warm meta-commentary here makes its appearance once again.

However, there is another crucial meta moment for attentive viewers in this finale. Nineteen minutes into the episode, Jane finds herself running to her wedding along the route of the Miami marathon. As she sprints through the crowd, she turns to a female course monitor by the roadside who quickly hands her a cup of water. The two women smile warmly at each other for just a moment. This is to my knowledge the only cameo in the entire series by creator Jennie Snyder Urman, and, movingly, it shows a kind of relay between Rodriguez and Urman, passing the creative baton from hand to hand. In "Chapter Ninety-Nine," the behind-the-scenes special that serves as a curtain-raiser for the finale, Gina Rodriguez says: "Jennie making me her Jane changed my life." Let us turn, or return, then, to this documentary episode, originally broadcast on the same day as the finale, which gives unique insight into the processes of *Jane the Virgin*'s creative team as they reached the end of their own extended race.

Creator Jennie Snyder Urman, boasting yellow nail polish that matches Jane's buttercup-hued dresses, is the only one of the professionals from behind the camera to speak, as this "making of" focuses on the actors. While Urman makes at the start brief reference to her series' roots in telenovela, she also stresses that "the central love story" is between the three women: daughter, mother, and grandmother. Some of the topics treated in the documentary thus coincide with the Narrator's opening voice-over to the finale (the family, the love stories). We also finally see the face of Anthony Mendez, Latin Lover, and hear him speak in his own voice, which is quite different from that of his familiar character.

Other themes are new. For example, the documentary celebrates the "unique visual style" of the series, as in its vibrant wardrobe and set design, so different from the dark and somber hues of many TV dramas at the time. This visual style includes the bringing to life via special effects of inanimate objects, such as fluffy toys or devotional statues, an example of the magical realism that runs through the series. Yet, beyond visual style, in this valedictory installment the actors lean into the political dimensions of their show. Justin Baldoni (Rafael) says *Jane the Virgin* reveals that "family is chosen, not blood" and proud Puerto Rican Yvonne Coll (Alba) cites the social implications of the abuela's immigration process at this particular time in the US. Yael Grobglas attests to her character Petra's lesbian love affair with JR as having a "powerful impact on people's [lives]." Andrea Navedo (Xiomara), also Puerto Rican in origin, laments that when she was a girl there were no actors who looked like her on American TV.

For her part, Gina Rodriguez remarks on how things have changed in the entertainment industry over the course of the series' production: "five years ago inclusivity was not where it is now." But she also praises the writers' room for facilitating a performance that switches on a dime from laughter to tears: "When you have great writing it's not as difficult a challenge to play those beats." The last episode of *Jane the Virgin*, the series that even future fans first thought would be absurd or ridiculous, thus gives rise to profound and moving reflections on aesthetics, thematics, and the politics of representation.

CONCLUSION

"You Will Recall . . ."

In the making-of documentary that serves as "Chapter Ninety-Nine," Jaime Camil (Rogelio) predicts that *Jane the Virgin* is "one of those shows that will never go away." The continuing contributions of the fan base, documented in this book, prove that this is indeed the case. In addition, after the show's finale, the creative team behind *Jane the Virgin* continued to contribute to female-focused TV dramas in Latinx media. Jennie Snyder Urman rebooted youth fantasy series *Charmed* (the CW, 2018–22). This new iteration featured three African-Latina witches in contrast to the original Anglo version. This casting choice exemplifies the commitment to diversity and representation in Urman's work.

Gina Rodriguez's post–*Jane the Virgin* career saw her taking on roles in cinema features across different genres, including the female-led apocalyptic science fiction film *Annihilation* (Alex Garland, 2018), in which she battles extraterrestrial monsters in a marsh, and the unique narco-meets-beauty-queen drama *Miss Bala*, a remake of a Mexican original (Catherine Hardwicke, 2019). Two more recent successes for Rodriguez hark back more closely to *Jane the Virgin* in that they combine the genre of romantic comedy with the theme of writing.

In her return to network series, Rodriguez plays a journalist in *Not Dead Yet* (ABC, 2023–24), a writer of obituaries. Here the magical realist themes of *Jane the Virgin* recur, as Rodriguez's character, recently split up with a boyfriend in London, returns to Los Angeles where she literally sees the dead people about whom she will write. In feature film *Players* (Trish Sie, 2024), a most-viewed title on Netflix, Rodriguez plays another journalist based in Brooklyn, this time specializing in sports, who is dedicated to artfully tricking casual hookups into bed. Her biggest catch is a celebrated and handsome British reporter, who, however, fails to support her in her work. It is no surprise that she ends up not with him but with her longtime best friend. He, like Rafael in *Jane the Virgin*, encourages and appreciates her writing. In both cases, screwball comedy and urban romance are combined with professional ambition in a way that Jane would surely recognize. The now-experienced Rodriguez takes an executive producer credit on both titles.

Yet some of Urman and Rodriguez's new projects remain in lengthy development, including a much-heralded reboot of the original series. *Jane the Novela*, described as "an anthology spinoff from The CW's beloved *Jane the Virgin* featuring star Gina Rodriguez as its narrator and exec producer," was the "lone pilot pass" on the channel in its season (Goldberg 2019). Meanwhile, the rightward political shift in Florida under Governor Ron DeSantis offers almost every day topical issues that I would love to see the original show address in its uniquely ironic yet warm way. The conservative, book-banning organization "Moms for Liberty" are countered by the progressive "Moms for Libros," a group that the literature-loving Latina mother Jane would surely have rushed to join (Rozsa 2024). Alba, now safely a citizen, would have been loudly indignant about the Miami radio host "who says he was fired for having a 'very Latino' show" (Chery 2024). Meanwhile, a recent book called *Teen TV* highlights our series' rare commitment to progressive causes like Planned Parenthood and immigration reform, even as the Target-shopping Jane pioneered what it calls "integrated product placement" addressed to the growing media market of Latinx millennials (Marghitu 2021, 171–72). It is a contradiction typical of the series, as it is of its protagonist and star.

As media and society continue to change, then, in the US and beyond, *Jane the Virgin* has become an enduring reminder of a now-distant era of free-to-air network television before the rise of streaming platforms. The five seasons and one hundred episodes "straight out of a telenovela" stand as a unique artistic achievement for their creative team and a unique comfort show for their faithful fan community, a true TV milestone that testifies to both the diversity and the artistry of recent US television.

WORKS CITED

Baldoni, Justin. 2022. *Boys Will Be Human: A Get-Real Gut-Check Guide to Becoming the Strongest, Bravest, Kindest Person You Can Be*. New York: HarperCollins.

Bentley, Jean. 2019. "'Jane the Virgin' Creator Explains That 'Fairytale' Series Finale." *The Hollywood Reporter*, July 31. https://www.hollywoodreporter.com/tv/tv-news/jane-virgin-series-finale-explained-1228182/.

Birnbaum, Debra. 2015. "'Jane the Virgin,' 'Shameless' and 'Glee' to Be Considered Comedies at 2015 Emmys." *Variety*, March 17. https://variety.com/2015/tv/news/emmy-awards-jane-the-virgin-glee-shameless-comedy-1201454753/.

Bolaños Medina, Alicia K., and Bélgica García Osorio. 2018. "El análisis de la variación lingüística en el doblaje de la serie 'Jane the Virgin.'" *Sendebar* 29(29): 81–107, November. 10.30827/sendebar.v29i0.6455.

"Camil y 'Jane the virgin' llegarán a México." 2015. *El Universal*, July 9, section Televisión. https://www.eluniversal.com.mx/articulo/espectaculos/television/2015/07/9/camil-y-jane-virgin-llegaran-mexico/.

Chan, Stephanie. 2015. "Gina Rodriguez Is Now the Co-Founder of a Lingerie Startup." *The Hollywood Reporter*, October 6. https://www.hollywoodreporter.com/news/general-news/gina-rodriguez-is-founder-naja-829862/.

Chery, Samantha. 2024. "A Miami Radio Host Says He Was Fired for Having a 'Very Latino' Show." *The Washington Post*, February 10. https://www.washingtonpost.com/style/media/2024/02/10/carlos-frias-miami-discrimination-complaint-latino/.

Cueva, Álvaro. 2023. "Las telenovelas en 2023." *Milenio*, December 29. https://www.milenio.com/opinion/alvaro-cueva/el-pozo-de-los-deseos-reprimidos/las-telenovelas-en-2023.

Dyer, Richard. 1998 [1979]. *Stars*. London: BFI.

Franceschi, Karla. 2015. "Juana la virgen regresa mañana en formato serial." *El Nacional*, November 18.

Friedlander, Whitney. 2015. "Gina Rodriguez Adds Spice to 'Crazy Ex-Girlfriend's' Tap Challenge." *Variety*, August 21. https://variety.com/2015/tv/news/video-gina-rodriguez-jane-the-virgin-crazy-ex-girlfirend-tapped-1201575666/.

Galarza, Litzy. 2022. "Alba the Undocumented: Immigration Law and Citizenship Excess in *Jane the Virgin*." *Howard Journal of Communications*, December 9. https://doi.org/10.1080/10646175.2021.2004477.

"Gina Rodríguez se disculpa por utilizar palabra racista en video." 2019. *El Universal*, October 16, section Espectáculos. https://www.eluniversal.com.mx/espectaculos/gina-rodriguez-se-disculpa-por-utilizar-palabra-racista-en-video/.

Goldberg, Lesley. 2014. "'Jane the Virgin' Star Gina Rodriguez Wants to Be the Latino Meryl Streep." *The Hollywood Reporter*, August 22. https://www.hollywoodreporter.com/tv/tv-news/jane-virgins-gina-rodriguez-wants-726918/.

——. 2019. "The Most Surprising TV Pilot Passes This Season." *The Hollywood Reporter*, May 12. https://www.hollywoodreporter.com/tv/tv-news/surprising-pilot-passes-season-2019-1209938/.

Hernández, Marta. 2006. "*Juana la virgen*—RCTV (2002)." *Todotnv.com*, July 6. http://www.todotnv.com/juana-la-virgen-rctv-2002.html.

Howard, Annie. 2015. "'Jane the Virgin' Star Gina Rodriguez: 'I'm a Brown Girl. I Have to Cross All the Lines Just to Be Known.'" *The Hollywood Reporter*, June 1. https://www.hollywoodreporter.com/news/general-news/jane-virgin-star-gina-rodriguez-798091/.

Huerta Ortiz, César. 2015a. "Camil trabajará con Britney Spears en 'Jane the virgin.'" *El Universal*, September 30, section Televisión. https://www.eluniversal.com.mx/articulo/espectaculos/television/2015/09/30/camil-trabajara-con-britney-spears-en-jane-virgin/.

——. 2015b. "La mexicana que da toque latino a 'Jane the virgin.'" *El Universal*, July 25, section Televisión. https://www.eluniversal.com.mx/articulo/espectaculos/television/2015/07/25/la-mexicana-que-da-toque-latino-jane-virgin/.

"Jaime Camil arranca segunda temporada de 'Jane the virgin.'" 2015. *El Universal*, July 3, section Televisión. https://www.eluniversal.com.mx/articulo/espectaculos/television/2015/07/4/jaime-camil-arranca-segunda-temporada-de-jane-virgin/.

"Jaime Camil seduce como Eva." 2017. *El Universal*, November 14, section Farándula. https://www.eluniversal.com.mx/espectaculos/farandula/jaime-camil-seduce-como-eva/.

"Jaime Camil y Silverman quieren producir cine y TV de calidad." 2015. *El Universal*, November 19, section Cine. https://www.eluniversal.com.mx/articulo/espectaculos/cine/2015/11/19/jaime-camil-y-silverman-quieren-producir-cine-y-tv-de-calidad/.

"Jane the Virgin." *Fandom*. https://janethevirgin.fandom.com/wiki/Jane_the_Virgin_Wiki.

"Jane the Virgin." *Tumblr*. https://cwjanethevirgin.tumblr.com/.

Jarvey, Natalie. 2015. "'Jane the Virgin' Telenovela 'The Passion of Santos' Gets Elaborate Backstory on Wattpad." *The Hollywood Reporter*, October 7. https://www.hollywoodreporter.com/tv/tv-news/jane-virgin-telenovela-passions-santos-830355/.

Loofbourow, Lili. 2023. "Seven Takeaways from the Netflix Viewership Report." *The Washington Post*, December 19. https://www.washingtonpost.com/entertainment/tv/2023/12/19/netflix-viewership-report-seven-takeaways/.

Lowry, Brian. 2014. "TV Review: 'Jane the Virgin.'" *Variety*, October 8. https://variety.com/2014/tv/reviews/tv-review-jane-the-virgin-1201322959/#!.

Marechal, A.J., and Anna Marie de la Fuente. 2012. "Latin Executives Vault into U.S." *Variety*, September 24.

Marghitu, Stefania. 2021. *Teen TV*. London: Routledge.

Melgarejo, Victoria, and Mary Bucholtz. 2020. "'Oh, I Don't Even Know How to Say This in Spanish': The Linguistic Representation of Latinxs in *Jane the Virgin*." *Spanish in Context*, December. https://doi.org/10.1075/sic.18028.buc.

Mérida, Janet. 2015. "Camil y Navedo presentan Jane the Virgin en México." *El Universal*, November 16, section Televisión. https://www.eluniversal.com.mx/articulo/espectaculos/television/2015/11/16/camil-y-navedo-presentan-jane-virgin-en-mexico/.

Miller, Sean J. 2016. "Making Diversity a Priority." *Backstage*, October 9.

Molina-Guzmán, Isabel. 2018. *Latinas and Latinos on TV*. Tucson: University of Arizona Press.

Monroy, Erika. 2017. "Jaime Camil no olvida su pasado en telenovelas." *El Universal*, February 23, section Televisión. https://www.eluniversal.com.mx/articulo/espectaculos/television/2017/02/23/jaime-camil-no-olvida-su-pasado-en-telenovelas/.

Moreno, Violeta. 2017. "Jaime Camil hace de 'Jane the Virgin' su familia." *Milenio*, November 14. https://www.milenio.com/espectaculos/jaime-camil-jane-the-virgin-familia.

Nguyen, Hanh. 2019. "'Jane the Virgin' Review: That 7-Minute Epic Monologue Is Everything That's Great About the Series." *IndieWire*, March 27. https://www.indiewire.com/criticism/shows/jane-the-virgin-review-season-5-episode-1-chapter-eighty-two-recap-spoilers-1202054006/.

O'Boyle, Michael. 2007. "Venezuela's RCTV in Gov't Crosshairs." *Variety*, March 26.

O'Connell, Mikey. 2014. "'Jane the Virgin' Showrunner Wants 'Ugly Betty' Meets 'Gilmore Girls.'" *The Hollywood Reporter*, July 18. https://www.hollywoodreporter.com/tv/tv-news/jane-virgin-showrunner-wants-ugly-719620/.

O'Hare, Kate. 2015. "NATPE Q&A: 'Jane the Virgin' Producer Jorge Grainer." *Variety*, January 16. https://variety.com/2015/tv/spotlight/natpe-qa-jane-the-virgin-producer-jorge-granier-1201406457/.

Orozco, Danielle Alexis. 2022. "Inhala, Exhala: Latinas, Mental Health Journeys, and Accessible Shaping Devices in TV." *Latinx TV in the Twenty-First Century*, edited by Frederick Luis Aldama. Tuscon: University of Arizona Press, pp. 113–42.

Orozco Gómez, Guillermo. 2001. *Televisión, audiencias y educación*. (*Enciclopedia Latinoamericana de Sociocultura y Comunicación*). Buenos Aires: Grupo Editorial Norma.

Parachuck, Tara. 2024. "What Is Vocal Fry and What Does It Sound Like?" *VBlog*, February 20. https://www.voices.com/blog/vocal-fry/.

Rose, Natalie. 2019. "Modern Melodrama: How the American Telenovela 'Jane the Virgin' Updates the Sentimental Novel." *The Journal of Popular Culture*, October 18. https://doi.org/10.1111/jpcu.12849.

Rozsa, Lori. 2024. "DeSantis Faces Pushback in Florida as Voters Tire of War on Woke." *The Washington Post*, March 9. https://www.washingtonpost.com/nation/2024/03/09/desantis-florida-woke-culture-wars-legislature/.

Ryan, Maureen. 2016. "All Hail Comedy's Takeover of TV." *Variety*, March 15. https://variety.com/2016/tv/features/comedy-takes-over-tv-1201725403/.

"r/JaneTheVirginCW." Reddit.com. www.reddit.com/r/JaneTheVirginCW/?rdt=41446.

Sava, Oliver. 2018. "Ivonne Coll on *Jane the Virgin*, Her *Godfather* Big Break, and Shattering Older Latina Stereotypes." *A.V. Club*, April 23. https://www.avclub.com/ivonne-coll-on-jane-the-virgin-her-godfather-big-break-1825377336.

Serafini, Dom. 2007. "RCTV & Government Woes; It's Déjà Vu All Over Again." *Video Age International*, May.

Shattuck, Kathryn. 2015. "'Jane the Virgin' Narrator on His Role and His Emmy Nomination." *The New York Times*, August 15. https://www.nytimes.com/2015/08/20/arts/television/jane-the-virgin-narrator-on-his-role-and-his-emmy-nomination.html?searchResultPosition=36.

Stanhope, Kate. 2016. "Inside 'Jane the Virgin's' Decision to Tackle the Abortion Question (Again)." *The Hollywood Reporter*, October 24. https://www.hollywoodreporter.com/tv/tv-news/jane-virgin-abortion-season-3-postmortem-940867/.

——. 2017. "'Jane the Virgin' Kills Off Its Star: Inside the Shocking Decision." *The Hollywood Reporter*, February 6. https://www.hollywoodreporter.com/tv/tv-news/jane-virgin-season-3-michael-dies-972648/.

Steel, Emily. 2015. "How Is U.S. TV Changing? Ask Jane." *The New York Times*, May 10. https://www.nytimes.com/2015/05/11/business/media/how-is-us-tv-changing-ask-jane.html?searchResultPosition=47.

Suddath, Claire. 2015. "In Her Prime: *Jane the Virgin*'s Minority Themes Have Made It a Serious Sitcom Hit." *Bloomberg Businessweek*, January 19. https://www.bloomberg.com/news/articles/2015-01-15/minority-themes-make-jane-the-virgin-a-serious-sitcom-hit.

Tabberer, Jamie. 2021. "Tyler Posey Comes Out as Queer and Sexually Fluid, Hits Back at 'Gay-Baiting' Claims." *Attitude*, July 5. https://www.attitude.co.uk/culture/film-tv/tyler-posey-comes-out-as-queer-and-sexually-fluid-hits-back-at-gay-baiting-claims-303215/.

Tartaglione, Nancy. 2019. "Propagate Sets Host of Local Format Deals for 'Jane the Virgin'; China, Korea, Israel Among Takers." *Deadline*, October 15, 2019. https://deadline.com/2019/10/jane-the-virgin-local-format-deals-propagate-china-korea-israel-egypt-greece-1202760271/.

Turchiano, Danielle. 2018. "Gina Rodriguez on Her 'Jane the Virgin' Directorial Debut: 'I Found It Very Freeing.'" *Variety*, February 9. https://variety.com/2018/tv/news/gina-rodriguez-jane-the-virgin-directing-interview-1202692816/.

——. 2019. "'Jane the Virgin' Boss Breaks Down Michael's Return in Final Season Premiere." *Variety*, March 27. https://variety.com/2019/tv/features/jane

-the-virgin-final-season-premiere-michael-jason-jennie-snyder-urman -interview-1203168910/.

VanArendonk, Kathryn. 2017. "10 Things You Learn from the *Jane the Virgin* Book, *Snow Falling*." *Vulture*, November 21. https://www.vulture.com/2017/11/snow-falling-jane-the-virgin-book-close-read.html.

Villanueva, Jane Gloriana. 2017. *Snow Falling*. New York: Adams Media.

Villarreal, Yvonne. 2018. "Gina Rodriguez on Her 'Jane the Virgin' Directorial Debut: 'I Can't Wait to See Where It Leads.'" *LATimes*, February 9. https://www.latimes.com/entertainment/tv/la-et-st-gina-rodriguez-directorial -debut-20180208-htmlstory.html.

Walker, Savanna. 2017. "Caridad Pineiro: Straight Out of a Telenovela." *BookPage*, November 14. https://www.bookpage.com/interviews/22048-caridad -pineiro-romance/.

"Which 'Jane the Virgin' Character Are You? Quiz." 2020. Needsomefun.net, August 10. https://www.needsomefun.net/which-jane-the-virgin-character -are-you-quiz/.

"#JanesHavingABaby." X.com. https://twitter.com/search?q=%23JanesHaving ABaby&src=typed_query.

INDEX

Note: Page numbers appearing in italics refer to figures.